THE END OF
WHITE
POLITICS

THE END OF WHITE POLITICS

HOW TO HEAL
OUR LIBERAL DIVIDE

ZERLINA MAXWELL

hachette
BOOKS

New York

Hachette Books
Hachette Book Group
1290 Avenue of the Americas
New York, NY 10104
HachetteBooks.com
Twitter.com/HachetteBooks
Instagram.com/HachetteBooks

First Edition: July 2020

Published by Hachette Books, an imprint of Perseus Books, LLC, a subsidiary of Hachette Book Group, Inc. The Hachette Books name and logo is a trademark of the Hachette Book Group.

The Hachette Speakers Bureau provides a wide range of authors for speaking events. To find out more, go to www.hachettespeakersbureau.com or call (866) 376-6591.

The publisher is not responsible for websites (or their content) that are not owned by the publisher.

Editorial production by Christine Marra, *Marra*thon Production Services. www.marrathoneditorial.org

Interior book design by Jane Raese
Text set in Linoletter

Library of Congress Control Number: 2020937827
ISBN 978-0-306-87361-4 (hardcover); ISBN 978-0-306-87359-1 (ebook)

Printed in the United States of America

LSC-C

10 9 8 7 6 5 4 3 2

Contents

THE END OF
WHITE
POLITICS

What Now, Liberals?

Los Angeles, CA—It's a hot summer day in July 2018, a few months shy of the critical midterms after the shocking 2016 election of Donald J. Trump. Two years of the Trump administration's chaos and hyperpartisanship set the stage for the fourth annual Politicon conference, where I was asked to speak on a panel titled "What Now, Liberals?"

This was my first time at Politicon, an annual convention in Los Angeles that has been a hub for colorful characters and the politically obsessed. It's a conference about politics, but think of Politicon as less of a stuffy meeting of political operatives and Capitol Hill insiders and more as a conference that represents the culmination of politics as reality show entertainment, where the green room can be populated by anyone from presidential campaign–winning political strategists like James Carville and Donna Brazile to flashy oddballs like Dennis Rodman, the cartoonish NBA Hall of Famer known for his colorfully dyed hair and a controversial relationship with North Korea. Why is someone like Rodman at Politicon, let alone standing next to conservative media personality Ann Coulter? I'm not sure, but the fact that the question even needs to be asked gives you an idea of the bizarre atmosphere. There's plenty of political cosplay, complete with red-, white-, and blue-themed outfits and people dressed in costumes of our founding fathers, like George Washington. It's a bit of a circus.

To be fair, though, Politicon is an equal opportunity circus. It has a bipartisan vibe, with activists and media personalities from all sides of the political spectrum, not to mention sideshow and carnival-barker-types looking for their moment in the spotlight. There are the bleached-blond Fox News wan-nabes, Tomi Lahren clones, and celebrity feminist activists, like actress Alyssa Milano, all there to speak their minds and stand out in the crowd, vying for the potential to snag a moment that goes viral on social media and earns them a coveted spot as the next cable news star or trending Twitter hashtag. The attendees are both obsessive political media watchers who want to get a glimpse of their favorite television pundits up close and political activists who are passionate about issues like climate change and getting dark money out of politics.

As a former staffer for Hillary Clinton's 2016 campaign, I was the perfect candidate for the "What Now, Liberals?" panel. I'm sure the original goal was to convene a bunch of bitter liberals to wax derisive about Donald Trump and point fingers of blame for the devastating electoral college defeat. The panel was moderated by Republican operative Shermichael Singleton and consisted of Daily Kos founder Markos Moulitsas, political commentator Sally Kohn, former Obama administration official Nayyera Haq, and Kyle Kulinski of the Young Turks network and the cofounder of Justice Democrats, a political action committee founded to run far-left progressive candidates against incumbent Democrats.

The Young Turks media network has a massive far-left following, and they were heavily populated throughout the packed conference center room. The audience was pretty rowdy from the start, interspersed with a littering of "Make America Great Again" hats and "Don't Blame Me I Voted for Bernie" gear.

The folks who show up to watch someone like Kulinski or Cenk Ugyur, the founder of Young Turks, are mostly male, mostly white, and always very vocal in their opposition to the Democratic establishment. The room is set up to spin the maximum amount of drama. About half of the room is solidly behind Bernie Sanders. To this segment of liberals, I'm perceived as a moderate because I worked for the Hillary Clinton campaign. The rest of the room is made up of Trump supporters who want to see liberals argue about why they lost in 2016.

After a few years on the cable news circuit and as a visible person who worked for Hillary Clinton, I was dubbed by my liberal colleagues and by this crowd as an overpaid shill even before I opened my mouth. Because of Hillary's history of taking donations from corporate PACs and high-dollar donors, she has been branded as a "corporate Democrat." Therefore by association with her, I'm caged under the same big-money umbrella. To be clear, big money in politics is a problem, but it wasn't a problem created by Hillary, nor was it one that Hillary wasn't critical of herself. As for me, I've never been overpaid, but facts don't seem to matter where this Politicon audience is concerned. This rush to judgment versus an impulse to listen is one of the reasons our Democratic movement has been challenged, and our own judgments often are what hold us back from winning as a party. To Kulinski's fans, I was viewed as part of the evil establishment. But as a black woman who is still paying off student loans, I think these so-called liberals need to get their facts straight, and I decided to make that panel the moment where I would speak my mind.

To understand the fervor and polarity in this room, you have to understand that the progressive left has traditionally separated into issue silos. And the Democratic establishment doesn't always lean toward or speak to each cause. So everyone is in a constant fight for attention around particular issues. There are the climate activists. There are the folks pushing for LGBTQ+ equality. There are those fighting for racial justice. But the truth is that all of these issues intersect, and most are also economic issues. They also all impact not just individuals but entire families and large populations.

Progressives have begun to understand this and to speak to these intersections of critical issues; for example, understanding that reproductive health care access is an economic issue for women and, by relation, entire families. As is equal pay, which is usually reported on as an issue only women have to care about, as if that woman's kids and spouse wouldn't benefit from having more money as well.

These silos exist in the progressive movement but more so in the form of divides. The intersection of race, gender, class, and sexual orientation is the place where the most work can be accomplished if policy makers of the future come to the table with an understanding that (1) lived experiences matter when it comes to informing effective policies and (2) not all lived experiences are the same, even within shared minority or demographic experiences. A white woman and a black woman are not treated the same in our society. Neither is a straight black man and gay Latino one. And it's in the mess of this disparate treatment that progressives need to focus on the future. Identity matters in politics. It informs the quality of our lives in some instances, despite the conservative mantra that every outcome is determined by a person's work ethic and drive. That lie has become exposed, especially as more and more historically marginalized people come into positions of political power.

Yet, it's proven to be difficult to imagine how we can utilize the party's diversity to rejoin our separate factions and move together as one powerful movement in the House, the presidency, and beyond. And that obstacle was evident in this room full of anxious Democrats I found myself sitting with at Politicon.

I'm sure the organizers wanted fireworks—and it was inside this three-ring political circus of Democratic schisms that they got their wish. The main source of the drama onstage was Kulinski, a Bernie Sanders supporter and progressive podcast host with a solid online speaking platform who came with a preprinted list of progressive policies he was primed to cite during the hour-long panel discussion. The audience made it known through their raucous applause for Kulinski whose side they were on. And it was not mine.

Kulinski's fans in the audience represent the id of some of the most vocal people on the progressive left; in many ways, they're the id of the Bernie Sanders supporter: white, male, Millennial, and uncompromising. Typically, these young white men, who love Bernie more than sliced bread, are also raucous, rowdy, and quick to heckle anyone deemed insufficiently progressive, the problem here being that anyone not named Bernie falls into this category for them. It was a no-win situation for me on that panel because I did not plan to go along with the status quo.

To be accepted by this camp you must pretend not to see any of Bernie's flaws, so for me the "What Now, Liberals?" panel was the perfect place to check the assumptions and refocus the conversation away from progressive purity tests. It was also the perfect place to establish the fact that the future of the Democratic Party depends upon people of color like me and to voice the fact that our perspective demands the attention of the entire spectrum of progressive politicos.

The future of the Democratic Party depends on confronting the persistent challenges we face as a movement as we continue to lack self-awareness about our own biases. But what ended up being manifested at this large Politicon gathering was a messy intraparty bickering match among Democrats. The real enemy and challenge for everyone in that room was defeating Republicans and Donald Trump, but you wouldn't know that based on my having to be escorted out in the end by security.

As each panelist laid out his or her analysis of what went wrong for Hillary and the Democrats in 2016, the crowd became more vocal, both in their applause and with their very loud booing of anyone who, like me, disagreed that Bernie's nonelection wasn't the source of today's Trump madness. As the conversation turned to what needed to be done to win going forward, I shifted in my seat to get ready to say what they didn't want to hear: "Future elections will be shaped and won by women of color." Then I added that all of the Democratic candidates would need to do a better job of speaking to and about the issues that black women, in particular, care about the most if they want to win the 2020 Democratic nomination—and that's why Bernie didn't win in 2016.

The crowd immediately reacted—and it wasn't pretty.

Boo! Boo! Shill!

I looked up into the liberal-minded crowd hissing and jeering at me, a bit taken aback by just how aggressive their reaction was to what I thought was an obvious point about Bernie's potential vulnerabilities. But nevertheless, I persisted. I didn't want to let this crowd of predominately boisterous Bernie Sanders supporters, still bitter from the 2016 primary, distract me from participating in the panel. We are all Democrats, after all. We are on the same team.

In reality, all I was doing was stating the obvious. Bernie's weakness among black women is well documented. I kept trying to make my point and back up my argument with data, like the fact that nearly a million black voters who voted for President Barack Obama in 2012 stayed home in 2016; in part, this disconnect exists because our party doesn't speak directly to those voters, including Saint Bernard. Clearly, the folks in this audience weren't familiar with the statistics.

"Bernie Sanders is the candidate best positioned to engage black women," Kulinski said. The crowd roared with applause.

Wrong. Sanders lost in 2016 because he got trounced in southern primary states, where black women gave Hillary Clinton the critical wins to amass the delegates needed to clinch the nomination. So, I immediately clapped back, "Bernie Sanders lost the primaries by four million votes. And so, while it is true that a lot of people still support Bernie Sanders, . . . he did not win the primary." And the truth is that it was older black voters in the South who supported Hillary Clinton in large numbers through the Super Tuesday states and southern primaries. Super Tuesday is the voting day in March of a presidential election year that's the closest thing to a nationwide primary. Nearly 40 percent of the American electorate vote on Super Tuesday—Alabama, Arkansas, Colorado, Georgia, Massachusetts, Minnesota (with caucuses), Oklahoma, Tennessee, Texas, Vermont, and Virginia. Clinton had amassed enough delegates on Super Tuesday to put her in a solid position to win the nomination. Months later,

Sanders would drop out of the race after the California primary on June 7, 2016.

I lived through 2016 with a bird's-eye view of it all and have the battle scars to prove it. I saw firsthand what worked and what didn't. And while everyone has something to say about the failed Hillary Clinton campaign, they usually don't include the fact that black turnout dropped 7 percent from 2012—and *that* largely impacted the election. And it isn't that most black people were just too busy that week. It's that the 4.4 million people who voted for Obama in 2012 stayed home, and a third of those people were black voters. The nearly one million black voters who decided not to turn out in 2016 would've likely tipped the election to Clinton. While in 2020 Democrats constantly want to talk about 77,000 votes in white working-class bastions like Wisconsin and Michigan, there doesn't seem to be enough media or party focus on the black voters. The last time I checked, 1 million was a bigger number than 77,000.

Boo! Boo! They continued to shout as I kept trying to speak about Bernie's lack of appeal to black voters as the major issue.

Booing as a silencing tactic may scare some folks into submission, but not me. What became clear to me was that the harassing and bullying behavior of the Democrats in the audience was just the in-person manifestation of a dynamic we saw during the 2016 primary and beyond.

I explained that there was a tangible impact on voter enthusiasm that took effect in 2016 that we have yet to deal with, and whether Russia expertly exploited already existing tensions around issues of race and gender or whether we simply acted out our own predisposed biases, we'll never really know. The voter suppression that led to a Trump victory resulted from many factors, but one that can't be denied is that the party establishment and the lefty types all contributed to the outcome as well because they weren't exactly doing a good job of engaging voters of color. That's because we are an afterthought instead of the central focus of the Democratic Party. Since the beginning of this country, whiteness and white voters have been analyzed, dissected, and obsessed over. However, the country is changing, and our politics must too.

After more heckling by the mostly white male audience later in the Politicon panel, I was outright frustrated. The moderator, Shermichael Singleton, tried to calm the crowd, but I was fed up with the disrespect. "You know what? Stop it!" I said. "There are children in cages. And if you guys are really progressive, we can work together to try to get this fucker out of the White House . . . [And the only way to defeat Donald Trump] is to engage black women."

And the spark for this book came in that moment.

In that Politicon room of rowdy leftist enthusiasts, what started as a fight among Democrats became a clarifying moment as I recognized the need to define the strategy for future Democratic success. That success is going to be built on a foundation of people of color who will need more than a few lines about free college to deliver their much-needed votes. We also aren't going to show up where folks are trying to yell and manipulate us into submission and aren't willing to listen, including to our feedback on their shortcomings. No one is immune from criticism, and to win future elections across the board and reestablish the power of our democracy, we need to start looking at the reality staring us right in the face.

The future of politics is not only going to be about what white voters want and think but will expand to include the ideas and needs of people of color who look like me. Our party will need to evolve to meet the demands of winning.

One of the things you should know about me is that I didn't join the Hillary Clinton campaign because I was a lifelong Hillary Clinton–obsessed fanatic. There were plenty of those amazing young staffers on the campaign, but I came into the fold with a sense of urgency to counter the threat of Donald Trump. I came to the Hillary Clinton campaign, post Barack Obama's success, knowing that people of color have been propelling candidates to victory all over the country since before 2016. Those same people of color, particularly women of color, are going to be an essential part of any Democratic success in the 2020 election and beyond, no matter who emerges the victor of the nomination.

I realized right there on the Politicon panel that I needed to make the case for inclusion. Women and brown people should now refuse to be drowned out by a traditional class of politicos who know only white male leadership. The end of white politics is about confronting not only America's blind spot for centering whiteness, angrily attacking anyone brave enough to point it out, but also understanding that the America of the future does not look like a whites-only club. It looks like me, and all of us. We need to listen to the people of color and diverse groups because that's who will bring us to the dance. We need to promote them to positions of power within our party. We need to listen to their honest assessment of how things have been done, where we've gone wrong with reaching voters who look like them, and let them lead the way.

At Politicon, the loudest voices in the room represented the fewest number of votes for the Democratic base—and they didn't even know it yet. I don't state this just because I happen to be a woman of color. Yes, I'm a black woman, and yes, I'm a progressive, but that doesn't mean I could fabricate an entire library of data and impartial analysis to support this argument. The facts are there. The movement is coming; the change is already happening. This is the end of politics as we've known it in America. We've been doing white identity politics since America's founding. We just called it politics. The white men booing in that room represent the past. They need to understand where we are going, so they don't get left behind. The women and people of color are already getting in formation, and we aren't going to be thrown off course.

Now that more perspectives other than those of white men are being considered, all of a sudden identity politics is a problem? The end of white politics is a statement of aspiration. It's one that acknowledges a country where we are able to radically rethink the issues and priorities of our government and to center the needs of every single American, regardless of their background, by focusing on identity-based politics. Unless we reimagine how we lay out Democratic priorities and speak more intentionally to diverse communities, they aren't going to show up for us at the ballot box. And why should they?

Unless you count booing as a type of persuasion.

CHAPTER 1

Demonized
Politics

I UNDERSTAND THE FRUSTRATION. In America, we participate in a political system that seems to benefit only those at the top and those who have always been at the top: white males of privilege. But we voters of color have frustrations of our own.

The party and the people in power have left us behind and forgotten about our most critical, pressing needs. The disconnect is clear when people of color try to pivot the political conversation away from a solitary focus on what white men want toward opening it up to what we all need. It's long past time for women and people of color to step out of the shadows of being an afterthought.

After Hillary's loss in 2016, there was a lot of criticism of identity politics because she amplified the historic nature of her glass-ceiling-shattering candidacy, basing it on being the first woman to ever win a major party's nomination for president. There were even some in our own party who criticized this messaging and criticized the entire idea of identity politics as a whole.

"It's not good enough for someone to say, 'I'm a woman! Vote for me!'" said Bernie Sanders. "No, that's not good enough. What we need is a woman who has the guts to stand up to Wall Street, to the insurance companies, to the drug companies, to the fossil fuel industry."

It's not only Bernie who has attacked candidates for highlighting their differences from the typical white male political option, as if the very prominence of this fact is a problem.

If it didn't matter that a candidate was a woman, then we probably would've had a woman president a long time ago.

We live in a world where being a woman does put you at a disadvantage from seeking positions of leadership and authority, and it's the obligation of today's politicians seeking power in 2020 and beyond to speak to that inequity as opposed to sweeping it away as if representation is a frivolous concern. Women need representation in politics because their perspective is much needed in American government. Every study shows that women are more likely to compromise when in office, and in doing so they are able to get more accomplished. We've come a long way from a country run by white male landowners, but you wouldn't know it by looking at the United States Senate. Currently, there are 26 women in the United States Senate out of 100 Senate seats: 17 Democratic senators and 9 Republican senators.

Currently, women are a majority of the US population. But their numbers in politics don't reflect that power in numbers. The Pew Research Center, a nonpartisan think tank based in Washington, DC, predicts that we are going to see a generational shift in our politics and that white people are projected to be a minority of voters by 2045. With demographics trending away from whiteness, the smart strategy as a party would be to prepare for the constituencies who will decide elections and shape the future. And those constituencies aren't white. America's coming demographic shifts put us on a collision course with an America that's long gone. I'm calling out African Americans, Latinx, and the LGBTQ+ communities. Identity-based politics—embracing identities other than those that are white, male, and heteronormative and running political campaigns based on the needs and experiences of those identities—are the future.

The term *identity politics* gets a bad rap from all sides, but it is absolutely the path to triumph for the Democratic Party. It requires an understanding of the intersectionality of all of our identities and how this intersectionality impacts our lives both individually and collectively. It was particularly trashed during and immediately after the 2016 presidential election. Senator Bernie Sanders made his disdain for identity politics known after the 2016 election, and he was part of a course of mainstream voices who insisted that Trump's win was the result of "economic anxiety" for the majority white voters who supported his election. Sanders has always railed against powerful monied interests and Wall Street but has only recently started to speak more to systemic inequality and racism. His dismissal of the importance of representation or why women want a woman president seems like an aspiration that is lost on the Vermont senator. When you've always been represented, as white men have, it isn't a top priority to ensure that others are represented too.

Fukuyama is cited by critics of identity politics who have said it's the catalyst for the social divisions we're currently experiencing in this country. The focus on lived experiences, Fukuyama says, "create[s] obstacles to empathy and communication." My view is exactly the opposite. I believe that people's lived experiences inform better policy making, and ultimately that is what we are doing here. Politics is about the people, and in order to take care of the American people, it is helpful to understand their needs, wants, and fears. Diverse representation means that those who are representing the rest of us in the government understand the communities they come from and aren't on a privileged perch looking down, defaulting to the perspective of white America.

The media defaults to the white America framing too— from print media to click bait headlines and right-wing TV. That's why they largely accepted this shared explanation about the ills of identity politics as a reason for Trump's existence in the White House. Most Americans swallowed this and moved on. But we shouldn't move on.

Merriam-Webster's defines identity politics as "politics in which groups of people having a particular racial, religious, ethnic, social, or cultural identity tend to promote their own specific interests or concerns without regard to the interests or concerns of any larger political group."

In response to Fukuyama, 2018 Georgia gubernatorial candidate Stacey Abrams wrote in *Foreign Affairs* magazine that the marginalized did not create identity politics. Instead, she explained that what Fukuyama saw as a "fracturing" is in reality "the result of marginalized groups finally overcoming centuries long efforts to erase them from the American political activism that will strengthen democratic rule not threaten it." What those who criticize identity politics misunderstand is that it is simply a description of politics that will now actually consider the concerns of diverse communities and promote their rise to the ranks of political leadership and power. Women and people of color cannot ignore their identity because it's not as simple as changing your outfit. You can't just take off your cultural identity or gender like a pair of pants. We can't simply choose to opt out of identity politics. I can't separate myself from my identity, and why would I? Our identities are part of who we are, and they impact how public policy improves or harms our daily lives. Our identities are part of who we are, and intersectionality matters. *Intersectionality* is defined by the *Oxford English Dictionary* as "the interconnected nature of social categorizations such as race, class, and gender as they apply to a given individual or group, regarded as creating overlapping and interdependent systems of discrimination or disadvantage."

It's the misunderstanding of what identity politics means that leads critics like Fukuyama to attack it as something distinctly different from the politics we've been playing since the dawn of American history. We've always been doing identity politics in America; it's just that up to this point in time, white has been the only identity that has mattered. We've defaulted to white as if that identity is neutral, as if it doesn't coincide with unearned benefits and a long history of divisiveness, trauma, and violence, as if white supremacy doesn't still exist in America. But identity politics isn't something that people of color can choose to opt out of.

It's helpful to understand this on a personal level. I am treated differently in a wide spectrum of situations because I am a black woman. Stereotypes about how black women are angry and hostile follow me everywhere I go, whether warranted or not, whether I personally display those personality traits or not, and whether those personality traits are justifiable or not. Black women and white women do not have the same lived experiences. When I walk into a job interview, every single stereotype about the people who share my race and gender walks into the room with me. Unfortunately, for people of color living in a culture where whiteness is considered better and more desired, we are at an automatic disadvantage in many circumstances, even if we are interacting with "good" people who "don't intend" to display bias. Implicit bias is something everyone has because we all grew up in the same culture. Our identity is not always something we can choose, and yet as a result, we don't get to choose whether we are treated better or worse for it either.

Identity politics is not something that marginalized communities can ignore; it must be at the center of their politics. They cannot ignore their own oppression in order to make it more comfortable for white Americans to engage. To gain equality, they must take on the structures that discriminate against them. To have it any other way would be to ignore the American experience we live.

One of the most important things we have to remember about identity politics is that it essentially creates a broader spectrum of politics, a framework that establishes new parameters for the people whose issues we consider and the person who is elected to represent those interests. Equal pay is an issue that illustrates this point. The often-cited statistic is that women make only 77 cents for every dollar a white man makes. But that's the statistic for white women. Black women actually make only 64 cents on the dollar, and Latinas make only 54 cents. That disparity illustrates how race *and* gender can affect economic status, and thus, policy solutions must take that into consideration. No policy to solve equal pay can truly be effective unless every aspect of people's lived experiences is taken into consideration, and those differ depending on what color skin we were born with. I wish this wasn't the case, but it is, and we have to deal with it. What most detractors to identity politics fail to realize is that in 2016, Donald Trump ran on identity politics too—white identity politics. If not explicitly, he certainly ran on prioritizing the interests of white Americans over everyone else.

"Trump went against the traditional Republican platform by promising to expand government, to protect Social Security, to protect Medicare and basically to provide government benefits that white people wanted. . . . Trump's appeal is about whites wanting to feel like they're getting some share of government benefits and support. This is of course wrong: White Americans receive a disproportionate share of resources whether that's from the government or just the overall economic, social and political resources in the United States," Duke University professor Ashley Jardina explained in an interview with *Salon* magazine. Jardina defines "white identity politics" as "the group of voters who feel attachment to their whiteness as a thread of solidarity and belonging. . . . They feel like their way of life is being threatened and they feel like their political power and status are waning," meaning that their white identity politics are directly tied to the white resistance. So, how is Trump's appeal to white America through white identity politics different from the intersectionality-driven identity politics that this new wave of Democrats has run on and been criticized for?

What we have to understand and not ignore is that when Trump blames Mexicans for the ills of modern society, what he's really saying is that America is at risk because it's less white than it was in the past. When Trump says that we need to ban all Muslims from crossing the borders of the United States until we can "figure out what the hell is going on," he's implying that their presence here makes America less great. And by less great, he means less white. When Trump says let's "make America great again," he really means he wants to "make America white again"—a country where white reigns supreme in culture and in politics. Don't be mistaken: this is *his* identity-based political platform.

The real idea of identity politics is just saying that there is more than one experience to consider as we set out to solve America's most pervasive problems. It's the work of progressives to think well beyond America's "default" identity.

Yet, Democrats are more concerned about getting back voters they "lost" to Trump, which they assume are all white and all working class, at the expense of the present and future base. If Trump was able to turn those voters out with racist appeals and bullying bluster, on what planet is there a unifying message for both them and black people? Democrats don't seem to understand that the coming demographic shift will have an even greater impact on our future, even though they're the party better positioned to benefit from it. I want Democrats to let this fact sink all the way in: you don't need a majority of white men to vote for Democrats to win. White voters—particularly working-class white male voters—have become a collective obsession of the Democratic establishment since the 2016 defeat, yet the outsized focus on white voters does not correlate with their importance to electoral success, especially in the future where everything is shifting and voter turnout numbers are trending upward.

Here's a fun fact: Democrats haven't won a majority of the white vote since 1964. Republicans, and some establishment Democrats, still stuck in the past—often obsessive over a mythical swing voter who is probably white and who lives in the suburbs—misunderstand the electorate. They miscalculate the inevitable shift in power to marginalized communities who harness the power of their votes. So many of us misunderstand our history and our past, and these Republicans and establishment Democrats who haven't assimilated modern realities benefit from our lack of understanding of our racial and political history.

Until 1964, the Democratic Party was right alongside Republicans in denying rights to black people. African Americans didn't win full voting rights until the Voting Rights Act (VRA) of 1965 was passed. The VRA, coupled with the Civil Rights Act a year earlier, created an exodus of southern-based Democrats who switched parties. That civil rights switch marked a period in American history where all of our politics realigned, creating the political parties as we know them today. At the time, even White House adviser Bill Moyers acknowledged, "I think we just delivered the South to the Republican Party for a long time to come."

Republican politicians have been playing to this white anxiety for decades, even before Trump. Richard Nixon employed what is known as the southern strategy to coalesce white voters against black civil rights, using dog whistles like "states' rights," which often was a code for allowing states to continue racist policies that discriminated against black Americans, particularly in the South. It's not a shock that we are in a current moment where the president is talking about an invasion of brown immigrants, exploiting America's racial divisions because Republicans of previous eras did the same thing, just not as explicitly. They disguise their protection of America's racial purity in words that sound reasonable, like "border security" or "protecting the homeland." Republicans began speaking to a growing sense of white resentment without being overtly racist. What's clear is that this backlash was the result of anxiety over the growing rights and political power black Americans gained during the civil rights era. By the time Jimmy Carter came along to win without a majority of white voters in 1980, followed by Bill Clinton (1992 and 1996) and Barack Obama (2008 and 2012), much of this political realignment of post–civil rights had been solidified. Both Clinton and Obama won two terms without a majority of white voters. The civil rights era was all about the status quo being ripped apart and the fallout from those progressive actions, resulting in an expansion of rights beyond only white people. A true reconciling of America's history and how it shapes our politics today is essential in building the movement that will do the most good in the long term.

The white supremacist underpinnings of our society that resonate and impact us today go beyond party lines. Although the identity or makeup of the parties' membership has definitely flipped, partisanship doesn't really begin to explain how the white supremacist structure improperly influences members of both parties to stand still and do nothing other than maintain a status quo that keeps them in office. And the demographics are continuing to shift in real time right under our feet, making it more and more likely that any success must be built on an identity-based formula rather than outdated traditions of the past.

America has had moments of progress that have rocked the very foundation of the white supremacist mind-set that's often prevalent in our country. Yet, it's important to remember that this progress often comes with backlash as well, such as we saw during the 2016 presidential election. The backlash, now often called "whitelash" by political pundits, to the first black president, Barack Obama, fueled the election of

Donald J. Trump as president. Whitelash is the breakdown of white identity politics; it was the result of an increased racial solidarity among white people with the shared perception that they were losing something—status, rights, and privileges—they had traditionally enjoyed. Trump, then, in many ways is uniquely American. Trump isn't the backlash; he is the response to the backlash. And in some ways, he's the manifestation of America's white supremacist soul, the dark underbelly that slaughtered Native Americans, kidnapped and enslaved Africans, and caged Latinx asylum seekers after separating parents from children. But joining our intersecting interests can combat this far easier than trying to go it alone, and the younger generations of Democrats are now embracing this fact, even though the establishment Dems aren't.

Fun fact number two: This wasn't the first time America snapped backward politically after making historic gains in the form of diverse representation. The highest number of black officials in history actually happened during the period from 1863 to 1877, the era known as Reconstruction. But with that progress came a white backlash, just as we've seen in this post-Obama era, and after Reconstruction ended, that period of racial and political progression was followed by decades of lynching and Jim Crow laws.

The political self-determination of black people in America seemed to be a bridge too far. Even today, the threat of another backlash is ever looming in the minds of establishment and moderate Democrats. Going forward, Democrats should not be afraid of this backlash from the faction of America still in favor of white supremacy, and they shouldn't fear identity politics just because conservative thinkers like

George Will or even Fukuyama say it's the reason we have a President Trump. That's ignoring the historical record and the reality. We've been playing white identity politics since the beginning, but this old way of doing things has left so many people and their concerns out of the conversation for too long.

How can black people be involved in politics if their representatives are not going to talk about police violence or the outright discrimination that keeps them from moving up the socioeconomic ladder? How can more LGBTQ+ people engage in politics without talking about the fact that they could be fired from their jobs or assaulted in the streets just because they aren't heterosexual? How can women engage in politics without talking about reproductive rights, disproportionate pay rates, workplace sexual harassment, and childcare struggles, especially if we are women who aren't white? It's the reason that childcare is not at the center of every single election at every single level. It's the reason that health care that men need is included in most plans but that birth control and procedures for reproductive rights were only recently added after a long legislative fight in Congress during the passage of Obamacare.

Republicans have touted identity politics as evidence that Democrats are out of touch with "real Americans," but that's not true. It's not a coincidence that the people who dismiss identity politics as a damaging framework for analysis happen to be beneficiaries of the status quo (read: heterosexual white men). So, let's think about identity politics this way: it's the framework that allows everyone to participate in a functioning democracy on a level playing field. We need to nominate candidates who have internalized the message that people of color will determine election outcomes and should be invested in immediately and that once we do we shouldn't look back as a party.

The fact that Republicans get this is giving them a head start. They aren't implementing laws that suppress the votes of communities of color for no reason. They are implementing voter ID laws that make it harder to vote because white voters are going to be a minority of voters. They are suppressing the votes of voters who are less likely to vote for Republicans, now or in the future, because they know that, in general, when voting turnout is high, Democrats win. They don't gerrymander districts for the hell of it. Gerrymandering and voter suppression don't cause our divisions; they are the result of them. Republicans know demographic shifts are against them, and while demographics aren't destiny, they definitely give the Democratic Party a built-in advantage.

We need an all-inclusive identity politics because the old system isn't going to be sustainable with our new emerging majority. Knowing where the population is headed in twenty-five years' time, Democrats should build a movement around the majority of citizens fighting for equality for everyone. Both statistically and morally speaking, this movement is the right choice for advancing our country's politics and framework of laws into the future. We must create a more expansive vision for our politics that goes well beyond the limited agenda we've seen in the past.

The conventional wisdom is that identity politics puts too much of a focus on race, gender, and other labels. People may think that identity politics is just black people voting for black people because of their skin color or a woman supporting a woman candidate because of her gender. That's

not the only reason, but it is *one* reason: equitable representation does matter. To build the future, progressives should
coalesce around different identities and see where opportunities exist to use that to inform our policy making and platform. It's all about creating a movement that acknowledges
the need for specific policy goals while moving everything
toward a more equitable future. The days of having only
old white men represent a diverse population that includes
mostly women is soon to be a relic of the past, and let's face
it, the progressive movement is already a coalition of intersecting interests. The nationwide emotional responses to the
2020 Democratic primary after the exit of the last woman,
Senator Elizabeth Warren, demonstrated a yearning for representative leadership, a yearning to push us forward into
this new reality.

Some white people may feel threatened by this argument,
though, and I see the hesitation of the white Democratic establishment to fully embrace this new strategy of centering
identity-based politics in everything that we do. The bus tour
that DNC chairman Tom Perez and Senator Bernie Sanders
took after the 2016 election is a great example of this lin-
gering hesitation and reluctance to move forward. On this
tour, they went to white working-class areas in the Midwest
to try to win back those Joe Lunchbucket voters, a huge mis-
fire that shouldn't be duplicated because, while every candidate has to communicate a message to every voter, there are
some voters who are never coming back into the Democratic
fold post Donald Trump. It's the decision of the traditionally
white and male establishment leaders to invest in white voters versus the Democratic voters of the future, which they
shy away from, so they can pretend we still live in the status

quo. We don't live there anymore, and we shouldn't be afraid of the future. If our movement is built on a weak foundation, we won't be able to survive into the future as a winning coalition.

CHAPTER 2

Bernie Bros Exist and So Does White Privilege

IDENTITY POLITICS CAN WIN ELECTIONS and be used as an ongoing winning strategy, but the problem is that even white men on the left—those who share the identity of those traditionally in power and their right-wing counterparts—are resistant to identity politics but for a different reason. They see it as a distraction or a deflection from their *own* interests, which have always been the first discussed and the last forgotten in American government and policy making.

No archetype of today's liberal brand of white male politics is louder and more visible than the Bernie Bros. These white male Democrats are frustrated with the consolidation of political and economic power being pulled away from them, and they want us to know it. Their trademark unruliness reaches far beyond the confines of conference room settings like Politicon; it has spilled out into the mainstream via social media and beyond.

A Bernie Bro is a male supporter of Bernie Sanders who expresses that support by attacking any non-Bernie candidate both verbally and online. We met them in the introduction when they attacked me. These attacks were particularly aimed at female supporters of Hillary Clinton during the 2016 campaign, but now their self-righteous little tentacles have stretched out farther and wider to strike anyone who even remotely disagrees with Bernie's politics. It's not only women who fall into this category, but it's mostly women, and these gendered attacks can turn into ugly name-calling faster than you can write a tweet.

The *Atlantic*'s Robinson Meyer, who first coined the term, very accurately described them in an October 17, 2015, article,

"Here Comes the Berniebro": "The Berniebro is not every Bernie Sanders supporter. Sanders's support skews young, but not particularly male. They are just a very loud contingent of his support and probably the most visible. The Berniebro is someone you may only have encountered if you're somewhat similar to him: white; well-educated; middle-class (or, delicately, 'upper middle-class'); and aware of NPR podcasts and jangly bearded bands." Today, the Bernie Bros are most likely to be spotted in a "Don't Blame Me; I Voted for Bernie" shirt, with no awareness that their throwaway Jill Stein protest votes against Hillary Clinton tipped Michigan toward Trump.

That kind of obsessive support is what developed into the "Bernie or bust" theme that started on Twitter during the 2016 Democratic primary race. The gist of this narcissistic ploy was that if Bernie supporters didn't get their guy, then they weren't going to vote at all, or they were going to write in Bernie Sanders's name in lieu of casting a ballot for Hillary Clinton. And when Bernie didn't win the Democratic primary, ultimately coming up four million votes short, their resentment made headlines across the nation when they stayed home or voted for third-party candidates rather than sticking to their self-proclaimed Democratic roots and voting for the candidate who'd actually received the Democratic nomination.

In the 2016 election, this act of Democratic iconoclasm from the "Bernie or bust" Bernie Bros made Michigan the ultimate Democratic casualty of this wave. It became one of the three states that gave Donald Trump the electoral college, even though Trump's victory was equivalent to less than the combined total of votes for third-party challenger Jill Stein. In other words, there were more votes for Jill Stein in Michigan than Donald Trump's margin of victory within that state. In Wisconsin, voter suppression and, yes, the lack of voter turnout among reliable Democratic voters gave the state to Trump. The same was true of Pennsylvania, and this trifecta of states tipped the White House to our forty-fifth president.

The argument goes that white working-class voters in these three states responded to Trump's populist message, but it's also true that it was a perfect storm that gave us Donald J. Trump—and one contention that factored in, particularly among white men on the left, was the argument that Hillary Clinton was just as bad as Trump and that since Bernie didn't win, it wasn't worth turning out for Clinton either. One celebrity Bernie Sanders surrogate, actress Susan Sarandon, famously said that a Trump win might be good because it would hasten the revolution. As we've watched the news reports about brown children in cages on the southern border, I've wondered if she thinks about this statement and whether it contributed to anyone's decision not to vote in 2016 or to vote for Trump.

The most ardent Bernie supporters even went so far as to claim that the Democratic primary was rigged when Clinton won by four million votes, though all analysis shows that there is no way the Democratic National Committee had any such capability. For a short time, veteran Democratic Party leader Donna Brazile fed into this conspiracy theory but later corrected the record, walking back her claim that the Democratic primary was rigged. While the vast majority of Bernie supporters showed up to support Hillary Clinton, a loud contingent has remained steadfast in being as obnoxious as possible to anyone who doesn't pass their Bernie-only litmus test. It's fine to have a different view on policies, but the level of hostility aimed at other leftists has been staggering and divisive. If nothing else, they've gotten plenty of practice with deploying the worst insults in the book (think about a four-letter word that starts with a *c*) toward women who are supposed to be on "the same side" as they are. The c-word, the b-word, a shill, a sellout. Those are just some of the names that are hurled at women like me by the Bernie Bros on social media spaces because we worked for or supported Hillary Clinton in 2016. And it's not just women who worked for Hillary, it's women who voted for Hillary or, to this day, even women who dare to say a nice thing about Hillary Clinton in a public space. This isn't an exaggeration either. To this very day, if I criticize Bernie's decisions, my mentions and social media profiles are bombarded by angry supporters calling me terrible names my momma didn't name me. In 2016, it got so bad that there were literally millions of women in *secret* Facebook groups that supported Hillary Clinton. Those groups provided a safe space, free of harassment from the Bernie supporters who, throughout the Democratic primary, became more and more vitriolic.

Case in point: if I were to, say, call attention to the reality that he has great top lines about the structural changes needed to remodel America so that it doesn't unfairly benefit the rich and powerful but then point out that he often stops there and should push the argument further, I would be shouted down and harassed off all social media sites before I could even press send on the tweet. It's an ugly routine that repeats like clockwork. To this very day, if I criticize Bernie online or on television, my mentions and social media profiles are bombarded by angry supporters harassing me in an attempt to silence my Bernie dissent. When you get called out by *Say Anything* actor John Cusack for being a shill who hates Bernie, you realize that the conversation has, perhaps, jumped the shark into the absurd.

That's what happened one random Saturday night in September 2019 when a swarm of harassment came swiftly to put me back in my place after I somehow came to the attention of the star of all our favorite '80s movies, actor John Cusack. You should know this about me: *Say Anything* is one of my favorite movies of all time. I love that movie and the song "In Your Eyes." I love the teen romance that reminds us all of that first crush where we felt butterflies in our stomachs. Cusack played Lloyd Dobler, an unemployed kickboxer who falls in love with the movie's heroine, Diane. I've come to have a nuanced opinion of the film as a feminist writer who now looks at the famous window scene where Lloyd stands in front of his black muscle car, parked outside Diane's window, wearing a trench coat and holding a boom box over his head playing "In Your Eyes," while he looks up with sad puppy-dog eyes; I've come to find the scene creepy and stalkerish because Diane had broken up with Lloyd in the previous scene. If someone shows up at my house in the middle of the night, I'm calling the cops, but that's just me. Cusack went on to star in a number of romantic comedies, but his public political persona to this day has been progressive through and through, and in today's speak, that means he's with Bernie.

Cusack has millions of followers on Twitter, so when he mentioned me on Twitter I knew right away. The trolls swarm when someone with that big of a following quotes you on Twitter. In my case, this kind of targeting resulted in hours and hours of muting, blocking, and reporting. For everyone, it's a big waste of time, and for some, that doesn't even factor in the emotional toll. It's fine to be upset when political analysts with a platform criticize your favorite politician. What is not OK is for you to use your sizable platform of millions of followers and about 25 percent of the Democratic primary electorate to harass or generate a pile-on against a woman with a different opinion. It's a silencing tactic to be sure, but I'm undeterred, and after a few replies, I wasn't in the mood to engage. The entire episode only served to ruin Lloyd Dobler for me forever.

This random Twitter moment with a famous Bernie supporter isn't just a pithy anecdote. It caused me to be unable to use Twitter—which, frankly, is a platform required in my profession—for about seventy-two hours. Imagine this: I have to systematically block and report the harassers, and sometimes, they even migrate to my Instagram to drop a comment or proclaim "Shill!" or their favorite four-letter word that starts with a *c*. Some of them even could be mistaken for Trump supporters, although the hashtags or red rose emojis that coincide with Bernie Sanders supporters help me distinguish which side of the political divide is attacking me at that very moment. And these people are supposedly progressives.

My mother taught me to stand up for myself and anyone else who is being treated unfairly or who is not as powerful as the people doing the hurting. I'll be damned if I will allow folks who claim to be progressive to tell me what I'm supposed to support and which candidates I can and cannot praise or criticize. A black woman like me, aware of the history and aware of the shifting demographic trends, isn't about to be quiet because a white man who likes the senator from Vermont thinks I should shut up and get in line, and neither should any other marginalized voice.

The online trolls are just one aspect of the Bernie Bros phenomena that, in some ways, represents the left's version of the last days of white-male-centered politics. Sanders may not see it this way, but the anger they feel toward anyone who doesn't check off their arbitrary list of policy positions—which somehow always fails to include the specific concerns of women and, particularly, women of color—becomes more and more palpable, even as the memory of 2016 fades away into the rearview mirror. With Russia in the mix, though, we may never know if any or all of them are real people who are passionately supporting Bernie Sanders for president or if the majority of them are bots, but we know the impact of their divisiveness can be felt in the real world and online on social media platforms.

Now, imagine a political divide in our country so wide that Russia could fit inside it. In 2016, this polarity was amplified and exploited by the Russians to the detriment of a potential blue wave and the first woman president. Based on the reports of all eight American intelligence agencies, Russia attacked the 2016 election through systematic hacking and dumping, coupled with social media propaganda about Hillary Clinton that exploited the already growing divide on the left between her supporters and those of Bernie Sanders. This divide was exploited through the entire primary and through the convention in Philadelphia. When the first batch of emails, stolen from the Democratic National Committee, was posted online the morning of the first day of the convention, the result was chaos.

We didn't have a full grasp of what was happening at the time, but the fact that Russia was able to capitalize on this political rift in our country and party is pretty good evidence that we haven't fully confronted it or understood it ourselves. This rift, in many ways, represents the crossings of many other divides in society and in American politics, whether it be race, gender, class, or sexual orientation. In my view, the Bernie Bros are a manifestation of white male privilege, an intersection where the aforementioned identity traits don't often reside. They wanted Bernie, and no one else would suffice. But the alternative they got instead was Donald Trump, and we are living through those harsh realities even now. Caged children aren't concerned with the nuance of Wall Street regulation, but people are suffering because the Bernie or bust set wasn't able to see past their own preferences and prejudices.

Not much has changed in the past four years. The most remarkable thing about the Bernie Bros was their exceptional affinity for turning a deaf ear to Bernie's weaknesses, even though understanding these weaknesses and acting on them would make him a stronger candidate and move him closer to the win they were all desperate to see him get. Instead of listening to the feedback of people of color, they aimed to shout us down and question our motives in deploying a critique of Saint Bernie, like my experience at Politicon, without considering the fact that no candidate is perfect. And, simply put, they have mastered the art of being jerks about it. Right before the 2020 Iowa caucuses, feminists reported getting doxed—a practice where harassers release their personal information, like their address, online. They wished rape would happen to us. They told us to kill ourselves. The harassment ran the gamut.

The viciousness from the Bernie Bros camp confirms that more is at work here than a simple preference for the Democratic socialist from Vermont. Sexism is so pervasive that it's hard to prove in the context of politics because voters support candidates for a complicated set of reasons, both personal and cultural. But if gender isn't a factor in support, then why was former vice president Joe Biden the preferred second choice for the majority of Bernie supporters over the more progressive Elizabeth Warren running in 2020—even though her policies were more similar to Sanders's than Biden's by a long shot? And if gender isn't a factor in support, then why were the Bernie Bros so virulently against only female Hillary supporters? If we can't admit that sexism played a role in Hillary Clinton not becoming the president, then we aren't really having a serious conversation that considers the reality of biases that women, including women in politics, are facing. How many female presidents have you seen in the Oval Office lately, or ever? Some of the men on the left still need to confront the bias they have for women in positions of power, and the Bernie Bros are absolutely part of this demographic.

The presidential race to replace Donald Trump started with six women in a bid for the Democratic nomination, and unsurprisingly, the one who got the most criticism online from the Bernie Bros was the only black woman who ran: Senator Kamala Harris. Whether it's the lefty narrative that Harris is "a cop," or the smears about her record as a prosecutor, or the overall dismissal of her candidacy as serious given both her policy positions and background, definitely a different standard was being applied to her record versus others who happened to be white men. For example, Joe Biden wrote the crime bill credited with creating the epidemic of mass incarceration and Bernie Sanders voted for it. Why would Harris have been the only candidate in the race criticized for not being on the right side of criminal justice issues?

Sanders started his 2020 run doing a better job than he did in 2016, considering how class issues intersect with race and gender, but there were still moments when he came up very short. Although Bernie Sanders had great top lines about the structural changes needed in order to remodel America so that it doesn't unfairly benefit the rich and powerful, he sometimes left me wanting a more explicit message on how he's going to dismantle the white supremacist structure that deems someone who looks like me is less valuable in every way than someone who looks like him.

One example of the misogynistic tension that enveloped the Sanders movement was the campaign's decision to accept and amplify Joe Rogan's endorsement, even including him in an advertisement for Bernie's campaign. As the host of *The Joe Rogan Experience*, Rogan, who's maybe most well known for being the host of the reality show *Fear Factor*, has a history of transphobic, homophobic, racist, and misogynistic comments, which should have made his endorsement unsavory to the Bernie campaign, but this, apparently, wasn't the case. The reaction to the Rogan endorsement was swift. A lot of people responded by saying that Rogan's endorsement definitely wasn't one that Bernie should amplify. But the campaign defended the endorsement by saying that "the tent is big" on the Democratic side. This dustup, as the campaign headed into the Iowa primary, really exemplified the gender divide taking place in the party, which the Bernie Bros problem embodied.

The bottom line is this: if the Democratic Party tent for the future includes people like Joe Rogan, that tent does not also include women like me. Racists do not belong in the tent. We do not try to put racists inside the tent because the people that they are oppressing with their bigoted views are tangibly hurt, not just by the rhetoric but also by the policies that racists are complicit in or overtly support. The fact that constituents with this ideology supported Bernie and that Bernie then accepted and promoted their endorsement speaks to the fact that, in some ways, the supporters of Trump and the Bernie Bros are responding to the same perceived loss of privileges—privileges that they have been afforded for generations. Though these two demographics of supporters are very different, they were reacting to the same stimulus in the political air, this perceived loss of white power, status, and influence.

If Bernie, or anyone like him, wants to prove to be the right leader, then he or she must lead. Unifying the progressive left is part of the job of the next Democratic nominee and president, and that work begins in earnest right now. Bernie has improved on these issues in the past four years, but his supporters have not. That someone in his position could let this aspect of his base continue for years is a failure of his leadership, and it shows that sexism and harassment are not as important to him as restructuring banking policy. This lack of evolution illustrates why someone like him is not the right leader for a future where women and people of color are looking to take their places as equal members of society.

Progressives have got to learn from the past, and we have to be better than this because we *know* better than this. We can't accept any segment of our movement harassing people who have been marginalized and who are finally powerful enough to speak up and demand that their voices be heard. To be fair, Sanders didn't completely ignore the problem, calling the behavior of his own Bernie Bro followers "disgusting," but he didn't do nearly enough to stop the harassment either. During the 2016 presidential campaign, Sanders told CNN's Jake Tapper that he was aware of the problem and that "we don't want that crap," adding that his campaign isn't about that, and he doesn't want anyone who supports him to do sexist things. I wish they would listen to Bernie.

We may never know, with Russia in the mix, if any or all of the Bernie Bros tweeting at me or leaving insulting Instagram comments under photos of my mother are trolls or real people who passionately support Bernie Sanders for president. But, again, we do know that John Cusack is, in fact, a real person and so is Joe Rogan.

CHAPTER 3

The White
Resistance

WHEN YOU'RE ACCUSTOMED to privilege, equality feels like oppression. White privilege is a paradigm or concept many of us have heard before, but it's necessary to unpack what it means in relation to white identity politics. For some reason, Americans are still limited to the whites-above-all ideology when it comes to politics in America. To shorthand it for folks who don't have time to read bell hooks, author of *Ain't I a Woman: Black Women and Feminism*, among many others, everything in America is about white people. There's a reason for this, but it's not a good one. History shows the lens through which we look: bigotry and discriminatory outcomes have led us from the founding of this country to where we are today in the twenty-first century. And the continued motivation for this has been based in both an American and global history of white supremacist structures that elevate white people over everyone else and then reinforce their supremacy through terrorism, violence, economic opportunities, and culture. The white establishment's resistance to the coming shifts in America's demographic is something that is felt on both sides of the political spectrum. It's not just Republicans that are freaking out about people of color voting our way into politics, and therefore reshaping the American ideology; the Democratic establishment has shown itself to be terrified too.

When you've only ever known privilege, any righting of the ship to a course of equality for all feels like you're losing control of the wheel. White Americans' resistance to people of color attaining leadership positions is a reflection of their fear for what's rightfully coming our way—inclusiveness and not just one token person here and there but a full-on major-ity. Ignoring the privileges afforded by whiteness has been detrimental to everyone else and in recent history has, with the election of Trump, more than ever been exploited for the gain of even the presidential seat. Does anyone really think that a US president with no political or military experience whatsoever, who has proven to be a corrupt, philandering racist, and who has been impeached would be allowed to get away with this for so long if he wasn't white and a man? We know better than that.

And people are being hurt in real time. Ashley Jardina, au-thor of the book *White Identity Politics*, described it this way in an interview with *Salon* in July 2019: "For the entire history of the United States, white people have had the majority of social, economic and political power. There have been dif-ferent periods of time in which that power has seemed less secure or it's been chipped away at. This is especially true at present and over the last decade. . . . Of course there is the symbolic power, which came from the election of the nation's first African-American president, Barack Obama."

Immediately after Obama's election, the Tea Party wave and Trump-led birther movement sparked a rise in white nationalism and overtly racist political rhetoric, which Donald Trump came to personify. This "whitelash" to the Obama era rocked the nation with an unprecedented pres-idential pick and an ensuing cascade of surreal events that have left half the nation either outraged or scratching their heads. Whitelash was the result of an increased racial sol-idarity among white people with the shared perception that they were losing something—status, rights, and privi-leges—they had traditionally enjoyed. The visibility of racial justice movements such as Black Lives Matter and the first black president upended a political and social narrative that has been continuing since America's founding. This demographic of whites, who felt at a loss during the Obama era, have now found an intense solidarity with one another in a much more concentrated way than ever before. This increase in a unified white nationalist mind-set as a group of collective interests, namely a set of privileges and benefits worth protecting, becomes stronger with each cycle of the census. That Trump was able to and did capitalize on this tension at this moment in history isn't surprising. Signs of the white resistance can be found on both the right and the left. Again, in some ways, the supporters of Trump and the Bernie Bros are responding to the same perceived loss of privileges that they have been afforded for generations. Though these two demographics of supporters are very different in the way they cast their ballots, they are reacting to the same stimulus in the political air right now.

In my own political experience, I can distinctly recall a moment when I was on the Hillary Clinton 2016 campaign. One of my colleagues said to me, "What is the difference between white supremacy and white nationalism?" Completely aghast, because I assumed everyone would know that from basic history class, I said, "White nationalism is Nazis. White supremacy is the system we're living under right now. It's basically everything else."

In my delicate tone and simple explanation, my colleague really grasped what the differences were, but it was one of those moments where I understood that, as a person of color, the race divide is something that is at the top of my mind in every moment. It's not necessarily top of the mind for most white Americans, and many of us—no matter the color of our skin—don't even know the difference between them. White nationalist terrorism forces white people to think about race and racism. It forces them to reflect upon their own behaviors and how they have possibly contributed to a world in which Latinos are targeted while shopping in a Walmart and African Americans are shot down as if we are in a civil race war. But it's also a distinction that needs to be made in our media, our educational system, and in the mainstream culture. People need to know what they're up against in order to combat it.

White supremacy is the foundation of American society. From its founding, America has been set up as a system of white supremacy and antiblack discrimination that prioritizes the needs and wants of white people over nonwhites. Donald Trump didn't invent it, but he did perfect it with the help of our extremist right-wing media environment. This was most evident during the whitelash and white supremacy-fueled 2017 Unite the Right white nationalist rally in Charlottesville, Virginia. In this American race war, a line was drawn in the sand. As an American citizen, you are either on one side of the racial divide or are on the other. Whether we like it or not, that's a fact of our current times. After a white nationalist murdered a nonviolent protester, Heather Heyer, at the 2017 Charlottesville riot, and Donald Trump went on TV to say, "There were very fine people on both sides," it became clear that we had a president who stood on the side of white nationalists and the Ku Klux Klan and refused to renounce or rebuke them. The message to people of color could not have been clearer: "We don't have your backs as a nation. You are on your own." That message is a threat.

The summer of 2019 was just as clarifying. The rhetoric coming directly from the president repeatedly emphasized the threat of an "invasion" and spoke of Latinx immigrants as if they were an infestation. Rhetoric like this historically leads to violence being committed against the scapegoated communities in question, and a few weeks into the height of the racist fearmongering and media hype, real violence did occur. Finally, after multiple mass shootings targeting Latinx communities in Texas and Ohio, the Band-Aid was officially ripped off America's post-Obama race divide. And this Band-Aid will keep getting ripped off time and time again, not allowing the nation to ever fully heal, because we are in denial of our wound in the first place. Princeton professor Eddie Glaude Jr., while on the MSNBC show, *Deadline: White House* with host Nicolle Wallace, reflected on the moment and on our collective response, saying, "America's not unique in its sins, as a country. We're not unique in our evils . . . I think where we may be singular is our refusal to acknowledge them, and the legends and myths we tell about our inherent goodness to hide, and cover, and conceal, so that we can maintain a kind of willful ignorance that protects our innocence."

Glaude's observation that we collectively remain in denial about our true history is absolutely true. It allows us to repeat many of the mistakes of past generations to our own detriment—and to our children's detriment and then to their children's detriment. Republicans benefit from our collective lack of understanding of our own racial history—from the often-distorted versions of it taught in schools and from our own disinterest in digging into the horrors of the past. And this, too, is a mistake that continuously comes back to bite us. Trump has deployed the modern era's version of

Richard Nixon's racist Southern Strategy since the Obama birther crusade—which he launched before he even formally started his bid for the presidency. But without a foundational understanding of history, many of us missed this historical replication and simply moved on with our lives. Lacking a foundational understanding of history, Americans have fallen into a pattern of treating the vile and corrosive words of Trump as an anomaly, but the truth is that he's part of a longer arc of history.

Trump's 2016 campaign was chauvinistic, complete with on-tape admissions of him sexually assaulting women and his full-on demonizing of people of color by subtly scapegoating African Americans, Latinos, and Muslims as the root of America's problems. The reluctance of most media outlets to use the word *racist* when referring to Trump's words and actions enabled this rhetoric to continue and gain traction. Even though people of color could see and hear plain as day what Trump's motives and ideologies were rooted in, it was interesting to watch the media contort themselves into different shapes to avoid saying the simple words "Donald Trump is a racist." His 2020 campaign is even worse; having done away completely with any subtleties or dog whistles whatsoever, it is fully emblazoned in bigoted bombast. He is now just saying or tweeting the racist dogma out loud, shamelessly and brazenly.

He *opened* his campaign saying that Mexicans were rapists and murderers. He boldly stated that Muslims shouldn't be allowed to *come* to the United States, a country that was established as a place of refuge for people fleeing religious oppression. By the time he said that black people live in hell and have "nothing to lose" by voting for Trump, the racism had become normalized to the point where everyday people felt emboldened by it, no longer seeing public displays of racism as taboo or unseemly.

This moment in history has revealed that the mainstream media is just as ill-equipped as the Democratic establishment to speak the truth about racism in the Trump era. Donald Trump has normalized xenophobia and skin-color prejudice. This normalization has created an environment where it is no longer wrong to be a flagrant bigot. It took the media years to even label Trump's behavior racist, perpetuating the threat his behavior poses to our communities. The racial divide, it seems, infects all areas of the American political system—including the fourth estate.

Trump's message was effective because of widespread white anxiety. Now, to a person of color, this all sounds pretty ridiculous. We know what oppression really feels like. We know what it feels like to walk around in a body that is valued less than. We know that our skin color dictates our treatment, meaning that we are treated better or worse depending on how light our skin is. We know that in culture and politics, this disparity has real consequences. White Americans are not experiencing more racial injustice than any other ethnicity has experienced at earlier points in American history. That's not even a realistic way to consider the dynamics of how race interacts with our political system because racial prejudices against nonwhites have been imbedded in our nation's ideology and legislature since America's genesis. Racial injustice is something that people of color experience every day. White Americans know they aren't treated the way black Americans are treated. Privilege doesn't mean that you're a racist. It means that you are enjoying some benefits because of the color of your skin, and you've never even had to think twice about it. It's about the things you don't have to think about—that's the benefit of your skin color.

White privilege means that you won't ever have to live with the burden of biases and prejudices that can invoke danger at any moment, such as being shot by the police just because you are driving, walking, running, or existing while black—like so many people who have, sadly, become household names, such as Walter Scott, Trayvon Martin, and Michael Brown. It's the privilege of not having to wonder how the world sees you because you have skin that is white; it's the privilege of being able to set the tone and the policy for an entire nation's populace and think that's just the way it should be because that's the way it's always been.

Racism isn't necessarily something that white people think about on a daily basis, but the increased share of people of color in the electorate has created a moment where America's focus has finally been forced to address issues of racial and gender justice, arguably for the first time since the civil rights movement and subsequent legislature. Our increased numbers demand that the powers that be address racism and white privilege once and for all. This coalition of newly empowered voters of the Obama era along with social justice movements, like Black Lives Matter, has to some white Americans signaled that they are losing, when actually it's just society realigning to become what it is meant to be.

The end of white politics means new American politics that understands that the lived experiences of people of color and white Americans are different and inequitable in significant ways that need to be transformed so that America can live up to its founding promise of life, liberty, and the pursuit of happiness for all. There is no question that the lived experiences of white people and people who are not white are distinct. "Good" white people are fully aware of this fact, even if they pretend to look the other way and stay silent about it.

Academic Jane Elliott has established a phenomenal exercise to explain white privilege. During a lecture to white college students, Dr. Elliott proposed the following to them:

"I want every white person in this room who would be happy to be treated as this society in general treats our black citizens. If you, as a white person, would be happy to receive the same treatment that our black citizens do in this society, please stand."

[No one stands. Silence.]

"You didn't understand the directions. If you white folks want to be treated the way blacks are in this society, stand. . . . Nobody's standing here. That says very plainly that you know what's happening. You know you don't want it for you. I want to know why you're so willing to accept it or to allow it to happen for others."

Elliott's point is that white Americans know people of color are discriminated against in every aspect of their lives, from overt displays of racism to systemic inequality in education, health care, pay rates, and so on. Even the persistent racial wealth gap in this country is the result of generations of institutionalized discrimination that prioritized white people in housing, education, jobs, and even safety. Elliott is simply pointing out the veil of denial that shields most white people from admitting they see the benefits they get. It's the disparities in both privileges and basic human rights that even "good" whites aren't willing to give up.

In essence, what Elliott is nailing down is how white privilege functions in a society where white people can still consider themselves to be "good" people even though they aren't doing anything to fix a broken system that prioritizes only *their* interests. You may not be actively bigoted, but you're not doing anything to stop it either.

Ironically, whiteness itself is, essentially, a made-up idea, and it hasn't even been a constant one at that. Who could be considered white has changed over time, as more European immigrant groups, like the Irish and Italians, came to the country. At one point in America's history, the Irish and Italians were considered "inferior white races," but over time they assimilated into a larger construction in our modern society, which allowed them to be labeled as white. Of course, this bit of history is easy and convenient to forget when status benefits are on the line—which shows just how changeable and fickle this arbitrary skin-color system really is.

This collective white part of the American electorate has always had priority over others and, at some points in history, even codified the denial of others' political participation into law. Think Jim Crow. Think voter suppression. Generations have fought and died to push us toward a more equitable future where traditionally marginalized voices can be heard, but it's only now in modern history that their electoral power has been able to be wielded in truly substantial and significant numbers.

With that in mind, in the 2020 Democratic primary, the topic of reparations became a central part of the conversation. Reparations are, essentially, compensation for the living descendants of enslaved Americans. My ancestors—who built this country and who have never been systematically compensated by the government, which gained its wealth and power by exploiting our labor—may now finally have the numbers to make reparations finally happen. The question is figuring out how much to give and who gets what. The late congressman John Conyers of Michigan introduced the same reparations bill for thirty consecutive years in Congress with no success. Now, Texas representative Sheila Jackson Lee has picked up the mantle of the reparations fight in Congress, putting the issue front and center once again at a time when people of color may finally have enough representation in Congress to at least push for a floor debate. The fact that this topic hasn't, until very recently, been something that the traditional political establishment would be willing to even consider is a sign that the times, they are a changin'—even if the change is coming slowly.

This conversation, of course, upsets white people of all political stripes, both because it reminds them of slavery and because it's a conversation that explicitly talks about special benefits for a group of people other than them. Never mind that white Americans have been benefiting for generations with the wealth and physical land and resources they didn't work for—at least originally. There must be compensation for the families who built this nation and whose lineage is still reeling from the impacts of these staggering imbalances. Remember when the election of the first black president was supposed to mean we were living in a postracial America? So, this primary's focus on reparations is a long way off from the idea that the magical black man solved America's race problems. That postracial lie was instantly discovered to really be racial animas building up over time, ready to erupt from under the surface with the right combination of provocations.

These demographic shifts, which have breached the horizon and are now upon us, are leading us to the moment when,
by 2045, a majority of the US population will be people of color,
which will change the electoral makeup and enable people of
color to have a transformative political impact. This will be a
seismic shift in our political priorities as we've known them
because America is designed to let the majority elect those
who represent and speak to their interests. If the majority of
the country is people of color, then that refocuses the political
conversation away from the one perspective we've historically legislated from. It doesn't mean that white Americans
will be left out, but they won't be the only ones with a seat at
the table. People of color will be able to effect change because
the sheer increase in numbers demands that elected officials
listen to what we have to say. This is a new thing. And it's
a new strategy for Democrats to build upon a foundation of
people of color, one so many of them are still uncomfortable
with. A December 2018 Pew Research Center poll found that
46 percent of white Americans said having a majority nonwhite nation in 2050 would "weaken American customs and
values," compared with 18 percent of black Americans and 25
percent of Latinx. Asked whether having a majority nonwhite
population would strengthen American customs and values,
42 percent of Democrats said it would, while only 13 percent
of Republicans agreed. The discomfort with this idea is clear,
but that doesn't mean it isn't happening.

Simultaneously, women are also taking over as the most
dominant voting gender. Yet as noted, in 2019, even though
women made up over 50 percent of the population, they only
accounted for 25 percent of the Senate and 23 percent of the
House. That's despite huge shifts in population, which have

contributed to a number of "firsts" in states like Texas, which sent its first ever Latinx representatives to Congress where this demographic makes up the majority of eligible voters for the first time ever. Since Donald Trump's election in 2016, nearly three million people have registered to vote in the state of Texas, and nearly two million of those voters are people of color and/or are under the age of twenty-five. That is the kind of uptick in diversity in the electorate that changes legislative chambers.

As a result of this shift, America has the potential to become a much more progressive country. But nothing is guaranteed. As Indiana University associate professor Bernard Fraga put it in his book *The Turnout Gap*: "Demographics are not destiny unless they manifest at the polls. It is the exercise of the vote that will lead to political equality [and] it is in the exercise of the vote that minority political power falls short." But upon the election of the first black president, Barack Obama, in 2008, the American political experiment began to show some cracks that might let the interests of people of color seep through, all because voters of color were motivated and mobilized to get out and vote. President Obama won because of record turnout of black and brown voters, winning nearly 75 percent of Latinx and Asians while receiving a record 93 percent of black voters on his path to a second term, solidifying the fact that the Democratic Party can and will win by prioritizing voters of color. Any Democrat looking to succeed in this current moment needs to understand that an intentional focus on registration and mobilization of the very voters that are just waiting to be engaged is the winning strategy. How do I know? Because Barack Obama did it twice.

Now that the electorate is more forceful in directly demanding action, they won't wait around for moderation. For too long, moderation was seen as a virtue. Incremental change was seen as better than nothing, and communities of color supported leaders who professed a more "pragmatic" top-down approach. There seemed to be this idea that people who were moderate were more palatable to a wider swath of the electorate. That was when the electorate was mostly white, though, and this present-day shift in the electorate demographic will change the way we consider what is possible.

Moderate voters should know that moderation isn't the answer to white resistance because, if so, the aggressively bigoted will never be held accountable, which helps to perpetuate oppression. Democrats can't fight bigotry with cowardice. They can't placate racists in order to keep moderate or independent voters in their camp. Those voters are already gone if they support the Trump administration's systematic caging of brown children on the southern border. They're already gone if this president's antics and behavior haven't already turned their stomachs and pushed them away from him. And, basic human empathy aside, the future demands a courageous calling out of those who would continue to expand on the bigoted place America has been for the last four centuries.

In some ways, 2016 and 2020 are the same in that the traditional power structures are flexing in response to an awakening of this new American electorate—an electorate powered by women and people of color. The futile race to the center—this narrative that says that only a safe moderate candidate can defeat Trump—is often entrenched in the idea that this moderate must likely come in the body of a white man. It is one of the more offensive aspects of the Democratic response to the devastating 2016 loss. It doesn't just say that as a party we aren't able to move forward past the white-centered politics of the past, but it also fails to acknowledge the base that has brought the Democratic Party so many victories in the past and present.

Simple answers are easy to find. It's easy to look no further than your own nose for answers. But this simple answer that establishment Dems are so dedicated to—the notion that moderation will be key in 2020—is born out of fear rather than fearlessness and confidence in our platforms.

The argument for moderation assumes that the only person who can defeat Trump is an archetype of someone who has been president before. It's often framed as if moderation is easier than bold progressive action. Moderation isn't a strong response to the Trump administration's madness. Donald Trump and his criminal associates are inflicting harm on communities of color. The response to that existential threat cannot be incremental change or moderation. This moment requires bold leadership and conviction.

Being a moderate is not a virtue. Moderation does not pull us toward progress. Instead, it is a response grounded in fear of the unknown at a time when we know that the future is more diverse and that we must, therefore, expand the conversation. For example, we must cease to break down only the white voting bloc into, for example, white college-educated or white working-class voters, while broadly referring to the "black vote" and the "Latino vote."

We can now take a deeper look at these blocs of voters of color in the same way we have analyzed white voters, because we now understand that these two demographics also exist at every income level. That's an exciting development because our representation and legislative priorities can also diversify once these conversations reach the mainstream. Moderates must understand that the key to demographic wins lies in *all* our votes combined; the disinterest in voters of color can only work against us all, collectively.

So, while the specific policies supported by this older, whiter, and more corporate-backed establishment wing of the Democratic Party may starkly differ from the Bernie Bros' free college and Medicare for All one-two step, they are also still missing the moment—and the point. When a moderate Mayor Pete takes the Medicare for All label and then tacks on an "all who want it" to sound more centrist, it does a disservice to those who studied up to create the universal health care policy in the first place. It's not about asking for less. You don't get more that way. This kind of thinking contradicts the reality of what the Democratic Party now has the numbers to push for.

The impulse to be moderate at this moment feels like a manifestation of the white privilege that has plagued us for so long. It operates from a position of fear. Fear of change. Fear of pushing boundaries. Fear of losing white privilege for what is now a small part of the Democratic electorate. Moderation is outdated for our times and our intractable problems, and this rush to the Democratic center is futile at best.

The Privilege of Whiteness: White Voices Speak Out

The race divide in America stems from America's original sin—the enslavement of Africans, West Indians, and their direct descendants—which has consistently mutated into diverse forms of abuse and exploitation that always result in the subjugation of black and brown people through discrimination and bigotry, while providing social and financial privileges to whites. These inherent privileges of whiteness allow for the privilege of being able to ignore race and walk through life unaware of the challenges that people who are not white face. While this is an obvious characteristic and flaw in the Bernie Bros machine and the clear motivating factor of the Trump brigade, white privilege doesn't stop there, and it doesn't exist in a vacuum.

Senator Kirsten Gillibrand was a candidate for the 2020 Democratic nomination who knew this. Though she dropped out of the race after failing to gain enough traction to qualify for the fall debates by getting over 2 percent in the polls, she clearly articulated, understood, and openly spoke to the needs of voters of color through her understanding of white privilege.

In Iowa, Gillibrand bravely offered a teachable moment for all white people when a white woman asked her about her thoughts on white privilege.

The exchange went as follows:

WOMAN: I hear you saying there is a lot of divisive language coming from Republicans, coming from Trump, and that we are looking for ways to blame each other. But the Democratic Party loves to throw around terms like white privilege. Now this is an area that across all demographics has been depressed because of the loss of its industry and the opioids crisis. So, what do you have to say to people in this area about so-called white privilege?

GILLIBRAND: So, I understand that families in this community are suffering deeply . . . that is devastating when you've lost your job. You've lost your ability to provide for your kids. That when you put twenty, thirty years into a company that all of the sudden doesn't care about you or won't call you back and gives you a day to move. That is not acceptable and not okay. So, no one in that circumstance is privileged on any level, but that's not what that conversation is about.

WOMAN: What is it about?

GILLIBRAND: I'm going to explain. What the conversation is about is when a community has been left behind for generations because of the color of their skin. When you've been denied job after job after job because you're black or because you're brown. Or when you go to the emergency room to have your baby . . . if you are a black woman you are four times more likely to die in childbirth because that health care provider doesn't believe you when you say I don't feel right. Because he doesn't value you. Or because she doesn't value you. So institutional racism is real. It doesn't take away your pain or suffering. It's just a different issue. Your suffering is just as important as a black or brown person's suffering, but to fix the problems that are happening in a black community, you need far more transformational efforts that are targeted for real racism that exists every day.

So, if your son is fifteen years old and smokes pot— he smokes pot just as much as the black boy in his neighborhood and the Latino boy in his neighborhood.

But that black and brown boy is four times more likely to get arrested. When he's arrested, that criminal justice system might require him to pay bail. Five hundred bucks. That kid does not have five hundred bucks; he might not be able to make bail. As an adult with a child at home and he's a single parent, if he is thrown in jail, no one is with his child. It doesn't matter what he says: "I have to go home. I have a child at home; he's only twelve. What am I going to do?" It doesn't matter. Imagine as a parent how you would feel so helpless. That's institutional racism. Your son will likely not have to deal with that because he is white.

So, when someone says white privilege, that is [what] they are talking about. That his whiteness will mean that a police officer might give him a second chance. It might mean that he doesn't get incarcerated because he had just smoked a joint with his girlfriend. It might mean that he won't have to post bail. It means he might be able to show up to work the next day and not lose his job and not be in the cycle of poverty that never ends.

During an August 7, 2019, interview with Natasha S. Alford of TheGrio, Gillibrand told Alford that it's been an evolution of sorts. She didn't begin her political career with a comprehensive understanding of how black people experience discrimination in their everyday lives, yet she's taken time to listen and learn from her constituents of color whose experiences she realized were very different from her own. "Every time I talk to a black person or a person of color and they tell me their story, I think, 'Wow. That has not happened to me.' And it's because my whiteness protects me."

The thing Gillibrand and several other Democratic hopefuls did with their messaging during the 2020 election cycle
was that they took the time to talk about race whenever the
issue intersected with the policy impact. They understood
that the race divide in America influences every single policy
issue. Joe Biden and Bernie Sanders were noticeably lacking
on this front, and you could hear it in their messaging. Com-
pare Gillibrand's response to Biden's response on whether
he feels a responsibility to repair the legacy of slavery. This
head-scratching exchange took place at the ABC News Democratic primary debate in Houston, Texas:

> Well, they have to deal with the—look, there's institutional
> segregation in this country. From the time I got involved,
> I started dealing with that. Redlining banks, making sure
> we are in a position where—look, you talk about education.
> [What] I propose is we take the very poor schools, triple the
> amount of money we spend—from $15 to $45 billion a year.
> Give every single teacher a raise to the $60,000 level. Num-
> ber two, make sure that we bring in to help the teachers
> deal with the problems that come from home. The problems
> that come from home, we have one school psychologist for
> every 1,500 kids in America today. It's crazy. The teach-
> ers are—I'm married to a teacher; my deceased wife is a
> teacher. They have every problem coming to them. Make
> sure that every single child does, in fact, have three-, four-,
> and five-year-olds go to school. Not day care, school. So-
> cial workers help parents deal with how to raise their chil-
> dren. It's not that they don't want to help; they don't know
> what to do. To play the radio, make sure the television—ex-
> cuse me, make sure you have the record player on at night,

the—make sure that kids hear words, a kid coming from a very poor school—a very poor background will hear four million words fewer spoken by the time we get there.

Biden couldn't sound more different than Gillibrand on the topic of race. He's talking about record players and social workers to help black parents raise their kids—mind you, when that wasn't even the question he was asked.

Gillibrand spoke fluently about race all the time—even when the question wasn't explicitly about race. She did so with the kind of courage and conviction we need from all of our white allies and, equally importantly, from all of our political leaders. She was able to articulately break down the ways that skin-color racism works, the ways in which her white skin privileges her and her family, and how we can make communities of color a bit more equal. She's a model for how white candidates, and white people in general, can talk about race with credibility. Gillibrand came at the issues through an intersectional lens—the same lens that, if used by all of the left, could eradicate even the conflicts we have on the issues of gender and sexism. Unlike Biden, she showed an understanding of the complexities of modern society and the base of the Democratic Party, without any consideration of how white moderates would react to her comments—and she did so without cue cards or a teleprompter.

During the primary campaign, Biden always sounded like he was crafting his responses to appeal to a blue-collar working-class white voter in Scranton. This lack of clarity and awareness that Biden and other establishment Democrats demonstrate around race issues is so ridiculous; they won't be able to reach Millennials or people of color with that messaging. They don't understand the concept and intricacies of white privilege, so they're not the voice of leadership we need to get us past them. The inability of Biden, Sanders, and other white Democrats to even speak authentically about race and acknowledge white privilege is an Achille's heel that needs to be tested. At the same time, we've seen this movie before. America didn't invent inhumane treatment; it didn't even invent caste systems. But it seems to be the market leader in perfecting both.

This is the moment where we need to be clear about what's happening. We need our leadership to be clear about what's happening, and we can't act like the experiences that little black children are having are being felt and experienced by little white children. There's a reason for that, and that reason isn't a pretty one to look in the face. But that doesn't mean we aren't obligated to look into the mirror that is our society and change the face of what we present to one another and to the world.

The Audacious Privilege of Pete

During the 2020 primaries, Democrats struggled to grasp and maintain voters of color—rarely addressing this demographic of voters in their policy recommendations and campaign messaging. The result was a general failure to coalesce these voter blocs behind them and their cause. It's like a wake-up call for everyone—candidates and voters alike—when they realize that the candidates who appeal to white voters aren't always the candidates who are going to win. Not anymore. But while this reality is an all-inclusive certain truth for

American politics today, there is no better example of a disconnect with voters of color and of audacious white privilege than South Bend mayor Pete Buttigieg.

By Election Day 2020, Buttigieg will be just thirty-eight-years old—nearly half the age of some of his former Democratic rivals. By late fall of 2019, he was topping most Iowa state tracking polls, shocking the mainstream media establishment and offering them an underdog story in a moment when Vice President Biden seemed to be struggling to solidify his front-runner status. When Warren soared to first place for a few weeks after a number of solid debate performances, it was Mayor Pete whom the media latched onto as the alternative to Warren's progressive agenda and Biden's campaign of nostalgia to a pre-Trump era. It was pretty clear at the time that the media was going to fall all over themselves to coronate him the front runner—the youthful candidate with charisma and a certain *je ne sais quoi* that was a hallmark of his lightning-in-a-bottle candidacy early on.

While Elizabeth Warren was an older candidate in the mix, her history-making candidacy and her progressive platform put her at odds with the mayor who appeared dead set on playing his role as the younger and equally moderate alternative to Biden. Simultaneously, Kamala Harris represented a new era in Democratic leadership, centering her campaign around the issues and experiences of black women with decades of experience under her belt in the largest state by population in the continental US. Before coming to the hunt for the Democratic nomination for president, she served as district attorney and then attorney general of California, a state of forty-four million people. So how, pray tell, did these two albeit dissimilar but equally qualified female candidates end up on the same debate stage as a mayor who won reelection with only eight thousand votes?

The standards for these presidential hopefuls were not the same by any means, and such displays only proved that successful women have to go above and beyond, polling consistently in double digits, in addition to having lived the equivalent of three careers before getting taken as seriously as a white male with a fraction of the experience they have. His audaciousness is less a commentary on his age and the Millennial generation as it is that the standard we hold Mayor Pete to isn't the same as any candidate of color or female contender. And his apparent refusal to acknowledge this reality was part of how his white male privilege manifested through the primary.

And the audacity of this candidate only increased from there. At a CNN forum, in the beginning of the campaign, Mayor Pete talked about how he was going to get into the policy nuance "later," but he wanted to establish himself and get some name recognition. Now granted, he was right about the fact that not talking specifics early in the campaign allowed him to gain traction on the surface level. But the problem is that the whole time, candidates like Elizabeth Warren were cranking out policies, becoming defined as candidates with plans for everything, working tirelessly to back up their claims for Medicare for All and other legislation, while defending their platforms from zealous naysayers poised to attack. Why didn't Mayor Pete have to have a plan for everything?

As a thirty-seven-year-old running for president, shouldn't he have shown up with plans in hand saying, "Look, I know I'm young, and I have very little experience in public life and I'm running for the most important job in the world. But here are my ideas, and it makes up for my inexperience"? The wait-and-see approach was really an expression of privilege. White male privilege. No thirty-seven-year-old woman with limited experience could show up, put her hand up, and say, "Oh, but you'll have to wait and see what my policies are later." No one would listen to her. Not a single voter would give her the time of day.

So, as I sat and frankly assessed the candidates on my radio show or on political panels, I teetered on the verge of fuming incredulity. Is a thirty-eight-year-old mayor of a small town in Indiana, who won with fewer votes than the number of people who daily browse my local mall, really ready to be the commander-in-chief and president of the United States? Is he the person who this demographic shift is really shaping up to select as the leader of our future? Does he truly understand those communities of color whose issues are going to be at the center of the political conversation?

Sure, Mayor Pete surged in the polls early on, but only in states where there were no black voters. Consistently, he was pulling zero or at a high of only 4 percent among black voters. And yet he had the audacity to have no plan whatsoever. The fact of the matter is that he could not win the primary. If you have no voters of color in your camp, you might as well pack up and leave because, as I've said, Joe Lunchbucket just won't get you there on his own anymore. Mayor Pete was seen as the promise of the future, but his lack of traction with black voters was actually the result of his failure to understand the past. History dictates that a leader who will calm a nervous electorate in the tumultuous Trump era is a candidate who can speak to the issues that connect the generations and link us all across our differences. We should be questioning the experience of candidates like Mayor Pete the moderate just like everyone else, and we should demand accountability before we get too excited about an untested small-town political star.

Mayor Pete may represent the future with his youth and charisma, but his basic lack of understanding of how to communicate to diverse voters was a no-win situation. All I saw with Mayor Pete onstage was the lack of regard that men have for the work women have to put in just to show up and be heard at all, much less be taken seriously as a candidate running for president of the United States—it's a manifestation of white male privilege and entitlement.

The real challenge for any Democratic hopeful, including Pete, is longevity. He hadn't had any opportunities to prove himself on the big stage, and when he did have a record to show from his time as the mayor of South Bend, the communities of color there didn't have anything good to say about him. His firing of the first black police chief and mishandling of a police killing in the town put him on shaky ground, and he had no connection to the community to draw from to resolve the mistrust. During his speeches, he had no idea how to close the race divide historically inherent in our country.

The media often cited his education and military background—he's a Rhodes Scholar and fought in Afghanistan—while they rarely mentioned similar accomplishments of Democratic rivals Julián Castro and Cory Booker, both of whom have been mayors and the latter is also a Rhodes Scholar. Not only did he seem to get outsized coverage, but the acknowledgment of his shortcomings was considered an afterthought. Elizabeth Warren, Cory Booker, Kamala Harris, and Julián Castro all centered their presidential platforms on the concerns of black and brown communities. They mentioned those communities and issues in debate answers even when it was not a question at the debates, and they organized events on the campaign trail that focused on often-invisible and intractable problems like poverty and mass incarceration. The racial divide can't be closed by someone who is in denial that it even exists or who is clueless of how to speak about it. Pete's lack of experience with these communities and the issues that concern them the most were obvious in his campaign's stumbles. States like Iowa and New Hampshire are hardly representative of where the party is going, and the generational divisions in the party are intersecting race in ways that were becoming overtly visible in the 2020 campaign.

So, it's not enough just to be of the generation. Candidates must also understand the lives of people of color to come to grips with the disparities between the lived experiences of people of different communities and across generations. This understanding does matter when considering public policy goals. The end of white politics is our party's secret weapon to success, since our base is the very part of the population that's growing in strength and political engagement. Although this book ticks through a flurry of divisions that exist on the liberal side of the political spectrum, such as gender, generation, and class, the divisions we currently face with race are the most divisive and traumatic for our nation. It's the volatile fault line in our culture that roars at the slightest provocation and that has become all the more precarious in this current moment of Donald Trump. The notion that we would even take Pete's candidacy seriously under these conditions was offensive. The Republicans can feel free to stick with their no-experience candidate, but not Democrats. Now that we are living through that political nightmare, Democrats understand that we need someone who has a vision for the future and know-how based on an awareness of the present. To women and communities of color, Buttigieg's sense of entitlement was unwelcome, and his lack of action on behalf of people of color was his downfall.

CHAPTER 4

The Obama Coalition

W̲E̲ ̲A̲L̲L̲ ̲K̲N̲O̲W̲ ̲W̲H̲E̲R̲E̲ ̲W̲E̲ ̲W̲E̲R̲E̲ when they called the
election in 2008. For Democrats, it's the modern-
day version of "Where were you when Kennedy
was shot?" I was bleary-eyed and crying on the phone with
my mom, the daughter of a civil rights activist of the Martin
Luther King Jr. era, yelling joyfully about how we had done it.
We had elected a black man to the highest office in America.

But who was the Obama coalition, exactly? This term is
frequently name-dropped when referring to that election
but remains an expression shrouded in a nostalgia of another time—an era that ended with the election of Donald
Trump. You may think of this coalition as the crowds of as-
sembled marchers who raised their fists in the air and yelled
loudly "Yes, we can!" or the people who knocked on doors
for months leading up to Obama's primary election. Those
2008 and 2012 Barack Obama supporters, whom journalists
and pollsters quickly dubbed "the Obama coalition" in his
first run for president, were all of that—while also not necessarily being any of that. Those voters didn't have to march
or door knock to gain such an emblematic label. Here's who
they really were: a combination of people of color, progressives, Millennials, Gen Xers, and previously sporadic voters
who recognized change on the horizon of the Democratic
Party and banded together at the polls to vote Obama into
the White House for two straight terms, defeating both John
McCain and Mitt Romney.

When news outlets say that so-and-so is up in the polls,
they're tracking and referring to a collection of "likely voters,"
a group of people who always vote and who are expected to

vote again. The Obama coalition's secret sauce was their ability to bring people out to the polls who don't normally vote—and to get them to do so in record numbers. In the 2008 Iowa caucus, Obama's charisma, progressive message, and promise for change brought out a younger demographic of voters, coalitions that created a spike in new voter turnout to a historic high of 58 percent of caucus goers who were participating for the very first time. Successful campaigns need to inspire, not just position themselves as the alternative to the opposing candidate, and Obama did just that, honing the potential for growth, long-term loyalty, and longevity of participation in the electoral process that these untapped voters offered.

I didn't think about going to work for Obama until the general election, but his victory in Iowa made his campaign worth following and worth joining to make sure I had a front-row seat to history. In 2008, I was home watching *Meet the Press*, with Chuck Todd doing a political analysis of the electoral map: he pointed out states on his board, some that lit up red and others, blue. The toss-up battleground states were marked with a striking yellow color, designed to grab attention and create alarm; they were something to watch out for. It was clear to me that not every state had equal importance in determining who became the next president. Having lived through the Supreme Court–decided election of 2000 and the devastating Democratic loss of 2004 at the height of the wars in Iraq and Afghanistan, I knew that I needed to go where my impact would matter to the outcome. The winner needs to get a total of 270 electoral votes to win the presidential election, and every election comes down to a handful of states—the battleground states—and the even more precarious toss-up states, which have historically voted both Democratic and Republican, depending on the election year.

I went on the Obama campaign website and looked for the link to apply for jobs. I used the online form to send my résumé to two yellow states, Pennsylvania and Virginia. I decided to start with yellow states on the map because they seemed the most challenging. If I was going to go and dedicate all my time to a presidential campaign, I might as well make some history and ensure an electoral college win in the process. The state of Virginia was particularly appealing to me, both because I had extended family there and because a Democrat had not won the state in a presidential election in forty-four years. If we could win Virginia and elect the first black president, then we would be making history twice over. I took a year off from law school to dive into the mission. My experience on the 2008 campaign changed the trajectory of my life forever. What could have been a life of legal briefs and depositions became a life of obsessive political engagement and a firm belief that my actions could make a difference to my entire generation.

And history was made. Obama's presidential wins were historic for more reasons than just the color of his skin: he also proved that identity politics work. In his two election wins, he showed that Democrats can still speak to and win those voters who are too often ignored in American policy—the voters who don't often hear a candidate's message tailored specifically to them and their lifestyle: working-class voters of color, teachers and domestic workers, minimum-wage employees, and the people who serve the rest of us. Obama's message of hope and change in 2008 was that we were the change we have all been waiting for. He also changed the way Democratic voters think about what their individual votes can do, showing them the power of the compound effect of putting all of the votes together to build a winning coalition. Young people and people of color who previously thought that their individual votes didn't matter, who weren't motivated enough to show up at the ballot box, combined their efforts on his behalf to accomplish a historic feat. Obama's presidential wins were the start of people of color and younger generations realizing the power they can grasp in their hands via their votes at the ballot box, and all signs pointed to this trend having the momentum to continue.

He was able to win over a veteran of the Democratic establishment, Hillary Clinton, which brought out traditional Democratic caucus goers demographically closer to retirement age. Obama brought in college students and middle-aged women who had never felt compelled to participate in the process before, setting off a historic run that catapulted him to two terms in the Oval Office.

In these moments, we realized and understood that the raw numbers were on the Democrats' side. If you don't go directly to young people and into communities that have historically been ignored by political power players, then why would those groups of voters have a reason to show up to vote for you? Targeting these folks with messaging they can understand and engage with is how to build the coalition you need to win.

Obama's election started and amplified a trend in American politics that is still ever-growing today—widening the separation between white voters with degrees and those without while expanding the influence of the African American vote. The echoes of this voter base still resound today.

Obama's election didn't *create* this trend but intensified it. The cultural tensions around race came to the surface in ways big and small but in no ways more obvious than when Donald Trump asked for proof that the first black president, with a name like Barack Hussein Obama, was really an American citizen. That narrative of Obama having something to hide or not really being one of "us" was a white-centered narrative that positioned America as a white Christian nation with everyone else an afterthought. With a black president in the Oval Office, this lie blew up in the faces of white men who had grown up with this ingrained belief system, including Donald Trump.

In today's United States, those who have higher levels of education tend to vote for Democrats, and those with less education tend to vote for Republicans. According to a 2018 report by Adam Harris in *The Atlantic* ("America Is Divided by Education"), the election of Donald Trump grew that divide in the education levels of voters, depending on their political affiliation, and this divide is more of a phenomenon with white voters: "According to exit polls, 61% of non-college-educated white voters cast their ballots for Republicans while just 45% of college-educated white voters did so. Meanwhile, 53% of college-educated white voters cast their votes for Democrats compared with 37% of those without a degree." In the election of Donald Trump, voters' opinions on race mattered more than any other factor. It wasn't economic anxiety that led some white voters to the Trump tent. Let's let that lie finally die. It was a feeling of racial resentment toward people of color—a sentiment that Trump vocally shared with them—that prompted these voters to rally around him.

This gap in education helps to clarify why this portion of white voters is so supportive of Republicans and Donald Trump when you consider what message they are being offered. It's a message of white dominance over everyone else and a rejection of the multicultural vision Barack Obama's presidency represented. Those who tended to be less educated gravitated toward Trump's ideologies and unsophisticated antics. It was a message that promised the world back into their hands and out of the hands of the "others" (nonwhites). The voters who are drawn in by racially divisive rhetoric and who have less education and exposure to a wider spectrum of people, ideas, and ideologies are more likely to fear a diverse picture of America. These voters grew up in a system of white supremacy and racism that Trump exploited to achieve a narrow electoral college win.

But the story heard most often about why Trump won had more to do with the so-called economic anxiety in poor white communities, particularly in the Midwest and the South. Manufacturing jobs had disappeared, people were struggling and in despair, the opioid crisis was in full bloom, and, according to this narrative, Trump was the only one to address directly this fear and discontent. In doing so, Trump tapped into and exploited an "us versus them" mentality. He even told the thousands attending the Republican convention in Cleveland in the summer of 2016 that he alone could fix it. The media loved this explanation—he's not pandering to racists, he's speaking to poor white economic anxiety—because it was a much more positive way to frame the conversation for voters. It was easier on the white mainstream media to land on an answer that absolved white Trump voters of bigotry while providing a reasonable explanation for how they could support Trump's overtly racist campaign. This tendency to provide a neat explanation caused us to miss the real explanation because it was an uncomfortable reality to confront.

The young voters that the Obama campaign reached weren't normally voters in the Democratic primary process. That's how he won the Iowa caucus. His campaign grew the electorate. Beginning with college students in Iowa, Obama used young organizers on university campuses to persuade students to attend the caucuses, an activity that candidates rarely invited young people to do. That's why the win was shocking. It's not only that Iowa, with its majority (91 percent) white population, voted for a black man named Barack Hussein Obama but that the polling going into the race said he would, an outcome that was fueled by these students. Looking back to what worked for Barack Obama with the coming shift in mind is the only effective strategy. The Obama coalition is still alive and possible, but only if Democrats learn to harness it correctly.

When polling is discussed on the national news, look at the bottom of the screen. Most of the time the words next to the asterisks say "likely voters," which means that the only people being polled at all are people who have a high propensity to vote. According to Pew Research, a "likely voter" is someone who has voted in the past and plans to definitely vote again. The disconnect is in the communication between candidates and political parties, which too often focuses only on a range of those voters without any outreach to voters who have disengaged from politics altogether. Politics is about the margins, but it's also about leaving no voter behind.

Since turnout is usually around only 50 percent nationally, even in a presidential election, it's clear that we are leaving a

lot of votes on the table. Imagine a nation where the majority of voters are people of color and nearly 70 percent go out
and vote. The representation of people of color in our government would be greatly increased. Obama's historic and
exciting candidacy turned out black voters who finally had a
chance to elect someone who wasn't a white man as the president, and that kind of turnout can be duplicated with other
candidates of color.

Every American eighteen years old and up is a potential
voter, but if you don't speak to them directly and often, they
aren't going to feel compelled to leave the house when new
Netflix content comes out every single day to occupy their
time instead. Why is Netflix able to get their attention and
not politics? It's because the messages that Netflix sends are
literally tailored to their taste and lifestyles. Why shouldn't
politics be too?

When I worked as a field organizer for Barack Obama's
2008 campaign, the biggest lesson I learned is that direct,
human-to-human contact helps drive elections, the time a
candidate takes to show voters just how important they are to
him or her—and that contact is reflected in the votes. It's just
one of the ways that Democrats are superior to the GOP, who
spend most of their time on the phone calling voters; contrast
that with what the 2008 Obama campaign called the Neighbor
to Neighbor program. Neighbor to Neighbor was the digital
tool that organizers and volunteers used in states to recruit
and track volunteers and engagement as Obama grew his
campaign from a small army to a massive grassroots movement. The program specifically targeted undecided voters
and got them to engage by speaking to someone they knew
personally—a neighbor!—because they were more likely to

trust the political opinions and facts coming from a trusted source such as someone they knew. Obama didn't invent direct voter engagement or organizing, but he did apply what he had learned from his work as a community organizer in Chicago to his presidential campaign with great success.

We need to shed the wrongheaded notion that talking about politics is not something that should be done in "polite" company. We are past all of that. Black and brown people are still being terrorized by law enforcement, whether it be police departments or immigration officials, and the threat isn't theoretical; it's existential. It's a matter of life and safety for entire communities, and the voters who aren't directly impacted have to come to understand this lived reality of other people who don't look like them.

My time on the Obama campaign as a field organizer in Virginia was very different from my time with Hillary in 2016 where I spent every day as the director of progressive media in the campaign's Brooklyn headquarters, clicking away at my MacBook keyboard, hoping that our message was reaching our audience. Campaigns like to say they are doing what Obama did and "knocking on doors," but you'll notice that they usually aren't until it's already too late in the election cycle. These days, they do more phone banking than door knocking. The point of door knocking isn't to just engage voters the last weekend before the election in order to remind them to vote and make sure they know where to go, but to ask them, first and foremost, what it is that they need.

Dems should be looking toward untapped numbers rather than the Joe Lunchbuckets they assume abandoned ship for Trump in 2016. It wasn't the white working-class voters who flipped from Obama to Trump that the Democrats *really* lost.

To believe this ignores the fact that there are big cities in all of the controversial states Hillary Clinton lost—Pennsylvania, Michigan, and Wisconsin—with large black populations. It ignores the fact that the decrease in black turnout in Philadelphia, Detroit, and Milwaukee was *larger* than the margin of Trump's victory by a factor of ten, meaning that it wasn't the white working-class voters who abandoned them, it was the black voters who felt they weren't being acknowledged and so chose to stay home who tipped the vote in those states.

With that in mind, Democrats shouldn't focus on voters who tolerate Trump's policies toward disenfranchised communities, such as the child separation policy, which snatches children from their parents as official policy, or Democratic candidate Mike Bloomberg's stop-and-frisk policy, which Trump supports and which disproportionately targets black and brown people, putting tons of them in prison. Where did these ideologies or policies originate? Definitely not in the black community. The stakes could not be higher for these communities, and these communities—as we proved in the 2020 South Carolina primary—are the bedrock of the Democratic Party. Black communities know not only economic pain but the physical, emotional, and psychological pain that comes with discriminatory and violent policies that abuse so many communities of color. The policies aren't just abstract policy debates for conversation. These policy outcomes impact real people: uncles, cousins, fathers, mothers. Elections provide the advantage of moral clarity of being either for or against the cruel treatment of people of color in this country, and now is the time for Democrats to focus on mobilizing those who understand this. Our people-powered democracy allows for those impacted to express their dissatisfaction, and the future allows for an expansion of political power. Now's the time to harness that.

As potential voters of color increase in numbers, their political power and influence increase. Even though all of the statistics clearly indicate that people of color are the crux of the Democratic Party, overall, these voters, at all levels and age groups, tend to engage too late in the election cycle, creating a "too little, too late" paradigm in terms of the amount of attention focused on what they actually want and need politically. This afterthought syndrome is losing Democrats elections. If the candidates running to lead the Democratic Party of the future don't regularly engage with communities of color, even when there isn't an election on the immediate horizon, they aren't going to gain our trust and enthusiasm. As Senator Cory Booker told me on my SiriusXM radio show in 2019, "You can't lead the people if you don't love the people." You also can't lead the people if you don't know the people.

I know from firsthand experience that Booker has gone out of his way for decades to know the very people he has been elected to serve. I was a student at Rutgers Law School in Newark, New Jersey, when he was the mayor. A fun finals break during my first year of night classes was to attend the community night ride patrols. Hundreds of Newark residents and students would meet at the firehouse to break up into groups of a few dozen per caravan, and we would go out into the community and "patrol" the neighborhood. This was a proven crime suppression tactic, and Booker had been doing them all by himself for a large chunk of his first term as mayor. His staff was concerned that he wasn't sleeping, so they suggested expanding the idea to include volunteers from the community itself to do the neighborhood watch. It was in those interactions that I saw of Mayor Booker with no cameras in sight that I grew to respect him living his values of getting to truly know the people.

It was this type of hands-on leadership I came to see as necessary to truly understand what elected officials and average citizens can do in a position of public leadership to help those in need. At its most basic foundation, that is what public service is all about. So, when Booker's campaign launched around themes of hope and unity, I wasn't at all surprised because I had seen firsthand, going back to his time as a city mayor, that he values human connection and understanding as an essential part of leadership. It's not just about flowery words and speeches. It's about getting in the faces of those that you serve and knowing their pains, fears, anxieties, and traumas. Representation isn't just about diversity of ethnicity but also about experience and empathy. Booker's presidential campaign centered around empathy and serving the people's real, lived needs.

When Democrats took back the House of Representatives in 2018, a historic number of women—118 in all, the vast majority of those Democratic wins—won elections all over the country because they ran campaigns that were authentic to their future constituents, just as President Barack Obama did. The candidates who ran were tailored to their districts—both on lived experiences and on the issues. These Democratic women responded to the needs of their specific districts.

A case in point is Lauren Underwood, who won the moderate fourteenth district in Illinois to become the youngest black woman ever elected to Congress in American history, and she did so by running on her lived experience as a black woman and as a nurse. With health care as the top issue for a majority of voters in those elections, her candidacy shines as a template for how to win by running on a combination of identity, experience, and policy specifics. The Republican majority in Congress has tried and failed to repeal Obamacare and strip away protections for preexisting medical conditions since Donald Trump was sworn into office in 2017. Underwood believed the incumbent Republican congressman, Randy Hultgren, who was then representing the fourteenth district, when he said he would ensure that protections for preexisting conditions remained in place, only to find that he had lied, like so many other politicians before him. Taking those protections away means that people who have preexisting conditions—which include things as common as pregnancy and as serious as surviving cancer—cannot buy into affordable insurance plans. This leaves them with less stable and more expensive alternatives. When Hultgren, who had previously said he would not vote to repeal Obamacare and these protections, voted to repeal, Underwood decided to run, challenging Hultgren. Underwood said, "Then I was mad. I'm not someone that thinks that my representative and I have to agree 100% on everything. But I do think that when they make a promise, they should keep their word."

Underwood's focus on health care led her to victory in a moderate and very white district populated by suburbs. With 30 percent of voters citing health care as a top voting issue in 2018, it's no surprise that Underwood's background as a nurse and her focus on preserving economic and health security for the constituents of Illinois's fourteenth district proved to be a winning strategy. Her win is instructive for future Democratic candidates in swing districts where coalition building is paramount.

Congresswoman Ayanna Pressley is the first black woman to be elected to Congress in the history of the state of Massachusetts. Pressley's campaign slogan, #WeCantWait, emphasized the need for a shift in leadership for Massachusetts's seventh district, a diverse, working-class constituency that includes the cities of Boston and Dorchester. When I interviewed Pressley for this book, she acknowledged how much pushback she got from the white political establishment about her focus on women of color. They wanted her to be less focused on women and girls of color; they bristled at her insistence that she wear her hair in Senegalese twists and traditionally black hairstyles. Her presentation needed to be more palatable to the white mainstream, especially in a city like Boston and a state like Massachusetts. Yet, her message prevailed because voters of color understood her connections to their communities and stood behind her. Pressley's unorthodox run focused on the fact that the systems that kept so many people down weren't invented by Trump. She made people aware that the focus on only certain segments of American voters, while others are ignored, is in need of a fundamental transformation. "This is not just about resisting and affronting Trump," she declared, garbed in a flowing red jumper. "Because the systemic inequalities and disparities that I'm talking about existed long before that man occupied the White House!"

When Pressley won and shocked the political establishment nationwide, she said, "I'm accountable in working for more than just who voted for me, but you know, each morning I'm thinking specifically about those who we effectively and successfully engaged or reengaged who had been ignored, left out, or left behind." The traditional white male consulting class didn't know what to do with an outspoken black city councilwoman from Boston who unapologetically ran her first race for city council on a message of protection and advocacy for women and girls of color. "I also had a multigenerational [strategy], you know, multicultural, every sexual orientation, gender identity—and that mattered. That informed everything. It's to ensure that you don't have blind spots." That's just never been done before in politics.

Politics, in this day and age, is all about blind spots because, traditionally, the people who craft our candidates' messages don't look like the people they are speaking to. They don't always know what it's like to be a victim of racial prejudice when they're crafting messages to communities of color or what it's like to experience workplace sexual harassment when they're crafting messages to women. We have not made it a prerequisite for our speech writers and campaign managers to actually *be* of the constituency that the candidate is looking to speak to, so it's no wonder that, even today, we're still hearing candidates speak in a way that doesn't fully engage all of their constituents. These messaging blind spots have created a need and an opportunity for candidates like Pressley to use their own experiences to speak directly to those Americans that share them, rather than just parroting what their out-of-touch campaign strategists tell them to say. That was her strategy, to speak what she knew from her own lived experiences—and from the lived experiences of those she was seeking to represent—rather than just listening to what her campaign consultants told her to do when she knew it wasn't right for her constituents.

Pressley's challenge of Mike Capuano, a veteran, ten-term incumbent, ruffled the feathers of establishment insiders. Incumbent candidates for Congress tend to win reelection 90 percent of the time, so any challenge to them that can upset the balance of establishment power is seen as an unnecessary annoyance to the party. Running against a reliable incumbent Democrat—someone who votes on policy the way the majority of Dems want them to vote, someone who's unlikely to challenge the status quo in return for being able to keep his or her seat of power—is normally seen as something that isn't worth the effort. You're probably going to lose, and for what? But Pressley didn't see running her campaign as something not worth the effort because, in her view, it's not just about voting the way the party wants you to vote, and it's not just about having someone in office who is a Democrat—a warm body who isn't actively working to help his or her constituents. It's about having someone who can speak truth to power and loudly advocate for constituents too at risk or too vulnerable to speak for themselves. Pressley's vision harkens back to the true meaning of representative democracy. In Pressley's eyes, "The people that are closest to the pain need to be closest to the power."

When Pressley announced her candidacy, the advice from some of the consultants was to play it safe and smooth out some of the edges to appeal to a more moderate and probably white electorate; she shouldn't make explicit appeals to communities of color by running on the protection of women and girls of color. She was told that identity-based politics wouldn't and couldn't work. Imagine all of the women of color who *needed* to hear that message, who were moved to vote for Pressley because of the truths she so bravely spoke in her campaign. She spoke about overcoming her own history of abuse and trauma to become an outspoken advocate for girls of color who were living through those same experiences— an unorthodox message. In a time when politics focuses on messages of economic prosperity, Pressley focused instead on the most vulnerable and unprotected people in her constituency, speaking out against physical abuse and speaking up for gender equality.

This all gets down to the systemic ways in which we come up with "the message" in the first place and how that system needs a complete overhaul. How will political consultants, who shape political candidates and their messaging, know how to speak to the people in the candidates' constituency when they *themselves* may not understand the people? A huge part of learning to harness this power correctly lies in learning how to articulate one's message to the people. Each demographic is different—they have different lived experiences and are searching for the fulfillment of different needs in public policy to help shape their lives. We are not a one-size-fits-all coalition, so a one-size-fits-all message is doomed to do more harm than good, alienating entire factions of the Democratic base with a single ill-fitted mantra or campaign slogan. Democrats need to be able to speak to men and women of color of all walks of life.

They particularly need to be able to speak to black women. Black women will play an especially crucial role in determining the election outcome in the 2020 Democratic primary race because, as *Fortune* magazine noted in a June 20, 2019, article by Melanie Eversley: "In the wake of the general election last year, black women stand out as a demographic group with one of the largest voter turnouts. The U.S. Census Bureau reports that 55% of eligible black women voters cast ballots in November 2018, a full six percentage points above the national turnout." That part of the Obama coalition also needs to be understood as a persuadable yet pragmatic bloc that *does* regularly participate in elections.

The key to harnessing the votes of any member of yesteryear's Obama coalition is tailoring a message to tackle the specific issues of the voter demographic while making it clear that they and their lived experiences are seen, acknowledged, and included in the mix of the political conversation. So, how do you harness and secure the votes of blacks, Latinos, and the younger generations? Here's a thought that rarely occurs to the Democratic old guard: What are the lived experiences of black and brown people? The simple answer is you have to first ask this question before you can realize that the answer is that it's something very different from the lived experience of a white male leader.

Often, data gurus on campaigns come up with a message they think might resonate with the most people based on feedback from focus groups that they set up to get a pulse on what the constituents are feeling. These focus group administrators are all well-meaning experts with stats and numbers, but that doesn't mean that they are actually *of* the constituency they're trying to learn more about or that they understand them beyond what is said within the confines of the focus group setting. Going forward, campaigns need to understand that cultural biases cannot be learned and accounted for within a single focus group session.

Using this focus group data, campaigns then poll the candidate's policy positions and messaging to see what gets the highest marks. But this ivory tower approach isn't the best way to win. Data can show only so much, and it can't tell law-makers what people are thinking and feeling. The Power-Point presentations and graphs don't reflect human impulses and biases like sexism and racism, which impact voting pref-erences and which are best spoken to through shared lived experiences.

This is why, as Democrats, we need to convene focus groups in real communities, not in manufactured settings, where candidates can get our feedback, or the candidates should be creating these groups. The listening sessions that these groups provide candidates and their staff are essential in opening up the line of communication between the peo-ple and those in power. But that line of communication often closes as soon as the data is collected or utilized instead of creating a feedback loop that persists as long as that person is representing the public. On campaigns, this feedback loop is necessary because political messaging needs to consider factors like bias that may impact the behavior and the needs of the people candidates are trying to reach and represent. Pressley's candidacy and model in Congress are a template for the future. She represents what is possible when the peo-ple in power have been through some of the same obstacles that they are in Congress to legislate against.

If the political strategists who are giving candidates ad-vice are not people of color and they are not on the election consultancy team, we need to look for a new lawmaker. Sy-mone Sanders, the press secretary for Bernie Sanders in 2016, was a senior adviser for Joe Biden in 2020. The cam-paign manager for Julián Castro moved over to advise Eliz-abeth Warren's campaign once he dropped out of the race. These people of color are advising candidates who haven't lived their experience but who want to understand it deeply so they can put forward workable policy solutions. Without the expertise of people of color, the plans these candidates hope to implement could seem out of touch with the constituency's lived reality.

The folks working beside government officials need to be diverse, as diverse as the voters the officials hope to represent, much like Barack Obama's and Hillary Clinton's campaigns were. I've been on the inside, and a lack of diversity in a candidate's campaign directly relates to campaign messages and whether they are in or out of step with the people. If you want a diverse coalition of voters to support your candidate, you'd better hire people who look like the coalition you are trying to build.

But there's no campaign school for little black kids. There's too little infrastructure in place to train young people of color to intern or work on a campaign, and young people who work on campaigns are better positioned to become future candidates. Democrats can gain a big opportunity and build up a pipeline of candidates if they work to include young people from the community in political campaigns. The old way of listening to a white man in khakis who has only seen the city of Baltimore because of the Stringer Bell character in *The Wire* is over.

CHAPTER 5

In Black Women We Trust

IT'S MY FIRST WEEK on the Hillary Clinton campaign, and I'm in the Brooklyn headquarters standing in an area of closely clustered cubicles with two black women colleagues, Denise Horn, director of African American media, and Ebony Meeks-Laidley, regional surrogate director, and we're catching up after the morning meeting. I hear a voice on the other side of the room yell, "The sisters are here!" A beautiful, smiling black woman is suddenly standing right in front of me. She throws up her arms for a hug. We hug even though this is our very first time meeting each other. We knew why we were hugging, and as our white colleagues mostly ignored the moment, clicking away at their laptops, that moment will always stand out in my mind as the moment I knew the black staff on Hillary's campaign were family. We were there to have one another's backs, but most importantly, we were there to speak for the people who look like us but who weren't able to be in the room to help elect a president.

That privilege was all ours, and we relished it every day, even in the hardest moments. Hillary hired Maya Harris, a veteran civil rights activist and former director of the ACLU of Northern California, as a senior policy adviser early on, so I knew that she understood how important black women were—not just as voters but as a brain trust to run a government. Harris would go on to chair her sister Kamala's 2020 presidential campagin. Her closest friends and longtime allies were frequent guests at the campaign headquarters. De'Ara Balenger, the Clinton campaign's director of engagement, would corral all of the black staff—or sometimes just the black women—in a small, empty office to hear from the black women who came before us, like the original "Colored Girls" (Donna Brazile, Reverend Leah Daughtry, Minyon Moore, Yolanda Caraway, and Tina Flournoy), a nickname the group of black women veteran political staffers coined during the 1988 presidential campaign of Michael Dukakis after they staged a small protest to demand more influence inside the Democratic campaign. We realized that these historical moments had opened the door to give us all a seat at the table on a presidential campaign, that they were the trailblazers who'd made it possible for the rest of us to have a voice as well. We understood that our legacies were tied and that we were there to advocate for women who looked like us.

Minyon Moore, a former White House staffer in the Clinton administration, always reminded me that I was there "to speak up for the people who look like me who can't be in the room" and in such close proximity to the people in power. We knew that for black women and families, we were their voices. The disconnect was that because so many media filters were obscuring our voices and presence, very few people even knew this about our campaign. Although it may not have been obvious from the outside, Hillary Clinton, a white woman from another generation, had a big contingent of Black Girl Magic all throughout her campaign. The inability of those on the outside to see us standing alongside Hillary— the first woman to win the presidential nomination of a major political party—is one of my biggest regrets and one of the biggest opportunities for future Democratic hopefuls.

Again, simply put: look for candidates who have campaigns made up of staff who look like the real America—diverse. If a campaign looks like the audience at the Country Music Association Awards, that candidate isn't getting the best advice.

We've too often marginalized and ignored this issue through-out history. For the next cycle and beyond, any Democrat who wants to be successful needs to understand who he or she is trying to reach and how. One out of every four voters in the Democratic primary is a black person. That means that anyone who wants to win needs to start with black people if they want to build a coalition based on a solid foundation of committed and engaged voters and citizens.

Shortly after the 2016 election, Higher Heights for America PAC (a political action committee dedicated to engaging black women in politics) sent a letter to the Democratic National Committee demanding a sit-down to talk about the issues black women are most concerned with. Higher Heights is the only (yes, the only) PAC in the United States that is committed to electing more progressive black women at all levels of American government. They endorsed Kamala Harris, the first black woman in the US Senate in two decades, and they also endorsed Stacey Abrams, the first black woman to win the nomination for governor in American history, to list a couple of accomplishments since Higher Heights founding.

The open letter said in part:

Black women have consistently shown up for Democrats as a loyal voting bloc, demonstrating time and again that we are crucial to the protection of progressive policies such as economic security, affordable health care and criminal justice reform. We have voted and organized our communities with little support or investment from the Democratic Party for voter mobilization efforts. Like civil rights activist Fannie Lou Hamer, who testified at the 1964

Democratic convention demanding blacks have a seat and voice within the party, we are "sick and tired of being sick and tired."

The Democratic Party has a real problem on its hands. Black female voters are the very foundation of a winning coalition, yet most black voters feel like the Democrats take them for granted. The party's foundation has a growing crack, and if it is not addressed quickly, the party will fall even further behind and, ultimately, fail in its quest to strengthen its political prospects. The Higher Heights' letter should serve as a handy to-do list for the Democratic Party.

DNC chairman Tom Perez did, eventually, convene these black women leaders to discuss the issues highlighted in the letter, but these concerns aren't ones that can be solved with just a few meetings. It has to be a sustained effort that allows black women, in particular, to set the agenda from positions of power right now because our voting power demands it. We vote at a rate that's a full 6 percent higher than the national average, so why wouldn't you want us in your corner?

Fortune magazine noted that, according to the US Census Bureau's Current Population Survey Voting and Registration Supplement, "just over 70% of eligible black women voters cast ballots in 2012, compared to 65.6% of white women, 62.6% of white men, 61.5% of black men and 59.2% of women of color overall." With numbers like this, it's obvious that black women are a key voting demographic.

And let's keep in mind, the truth is that Trump did steal away some of the black male vote. He represented the kind of brash and unabashed toxic masculinity that some men of color aspire to. No, not all. But yes, some. And we have to be honest about this dynamic within communities of color. Sexism and racism are a stew of bigotry, but they can both exist alone and manifest at the same time in many ways. Trump's misogyny didn't deter 13 percent of black men from voting for a man who said the first black president wasn't legitimate or even American. That's a lot to overlook if you live every day as a black man with the daily slights and sometimes egregious examples of bigotry and violence, but they did. And it's not a coincidence that the alternative was a woman named Hillary Clinton—that they would have rather seen a racist white man in the Oval Office than a woman speaks volumes. I do hate to say this, but some black men don't want all people to be equal; some want to be equal to white men and, ultimately, dominant over all colors of women.

Imagine this: Anti-black racism and bias isn't the only race-based discrimination that women of color face. Sometimes the call is coming from inside the house. We also face bias from within—a vestige of our black American history dating back to slavery. At the core of it all is always either the notion, actuality, or interference of white people. For example, during Kamala Harris's run for the 2020 Democratic nomination, some black men distrusted her: they saw her as not sufficiently loyal to the race because her husband, Douglas Emhoff, is a white man. I called out some of those black men on MSNBC for having an issue with Harris simply for being a black woman with a white husband, and immediately faced trolling from black men who love black women but who think the best way to demonstrate that love is to call me and Harris "bedwenches." A "Negro bed wench," according to online troll Tariq Nasheed, who coined the term, "was formerly an enslaved black woman on one of the plantations of old whose specific function was to have sex with the plantation's white owner, her master."

Though history has taught us that most enslaved African women were understandably horrified at the idea of sexual contact with their enslavers (and presumably all white men), some, Nasheed asserts, embraced this role and all the comparative privileges it brought. Worse, some Negro bed wenches even imagined that they were better than the rest of their enslaved brothers and sisters and used their, once again, *comparatively* privileged positions to thoroughly ingratiate themselves to their owners. The contemporary Negro bed wench mentality, therefore, is displayed when a black woman—suffering from Stockholm syndrome, according to Nasheed—accepts and even acts to further white supremacy. The Negro bed wench mentality, while still implicitly sexual in name, no longer requires a black woman to have sexual contact with a white person to manifest. According to Nasheed, she's the black female counterpart to Uncle Tom.

It's all pretty gross, and Harris has faced these kinds of attacks ever since her exchange with Joe Biden at the very first primary debate. Evidently, even black men have some work to do when it comes to uplifting the women in our own community rather than attacking them for dating white men or marrying them. The dripping misogyny isn't surprising. Black women face both racism and misogyny on a constant basis, and in this case, Harris faced criticism from white liberals and the mainstream elites for not being sufficiently deferential to Biden while also being criticized by black men for not being loyal enough to the black community. It's all personal and political terrorism toward a woman who dared challenge the status quo—in more ways than one—and it's appallingly disgusting to see this misogyny in these seemingly progressive times we live in.

Five years after Maya Harris's paper for the Center for American Progress declaring women of color to be a growing force in the American electorate, the organization followed up with another 2019 report that confirmed Harris's analysis: "Today, [women of color] are emerging as a potential electoral powerhouse—and they fully deserve elected officials' attention and respect." Black women in particular have an outsized influence on electoral outcomes because they don't just vote—they pull everyone in their entire household along with them to the polls and, in some cases, into activism as well. If you don't believe that, just ask Doug Jones.

Jones is now a Democratic senator in the bright red state of Alabama, not to mention a shining example of how you can recreate an Obama coalition simply off the support of black voters—even in a red state. Jones is a moderate who ran in the 2018 midterms against an accused molester of teenage girls, Judge Roy Moore. Moore was endorsed by Donald Trump, even after the allegations of sexual misconduct hit the mainstream, and Steve Bannon even flew in for an emergency campaign stop to save Moore's campaign from nosediving after the allegations became public.

But Jones had his own political trick up his sleeve. As the prosecutor who put the murderer of the four little girls in the Birmingham church bombing of 1963 into prison, he has a connection to the black community. In Alabama's special election, Jones won on the strength of black women not just turning out to reject the misogyny, abuse, and allegations against his opponent, Moore, but also because he had stood up for little black girls in America's court of law. Though he wasn't a member of the black community, he had a genuine connection with it, dating back decades. He didn't just show up asking for the black vote when it was convenient for him—as we've seen in most election cycles, including the 2020 race for the Democratic nomination—and he was able to use this to his advantage to build his own coalition of voters of color. With the backing of a Republican president in a historically overwhelmingly Republican state and without those black women mobilizing against Moore and turning out the vote in their communities, it's likely that Moore would've won. This is what the party is supposed to do, and we should look to these women as a guide on how to get the job done and build a winning Democratic coalition, even in a reliably Republican state.

While Jones was successful, his win demonstrates only part of the winning formula. The other part is that it was black women who brought him over the finish line. Although he did have a solid history working on behalf of the community, black women also mobilized on their own, knowing full well what Moore stood for.

What we really should be doing to rebuild this coalition—and what Doug Jones got right—is putting black women at the center of the conversation. Jones didn't do this late in the race just to get black women to turn out, and neither did Barack Obama. Instead, both these leaders showed a real personal investment in the community, and a history within it, to gain the sturdy trust of the black community and to mobilize their vote. It was Jones's authentic concern with and connection to the African American community that catapulted him to the win, rather than merely assuming that blacks would give him the vote just because he's a Democrat, as Hillary Clinton is accused of doing and as Joe Biden repeatedly did in the 2020 race for the Democratic nomination. Here, black women were the firewall that stopped a child molester from being sworn into the US Senate, and they trusted a man who had a deep connection to a painful history in the African American community. It's an example of how other Democrats can make these same connections by taking the opportunity to stand up for people of color when we are the targets of racism or racist policies. Jones stood up for the most vulnerable victims of color, even long after justice seemed elusive, and that's why his coalition trusted him.

Black women knew that supporting Jones against Moore sent a message to the Democratic Party that they are the base that can propel Democrats, even in a deep red state. They are a core foundation of the Obama coalition that Democrats are seeking to rebuild and proof that the strength of a renewed coalition can and will win elections, even without a majority of the white working-class voters that Democrats have historically eyed as the true ballot-box prize. Let's do the math: only 29 percent of the electorate in Doug Jones's Alabama race were black, but he received 98 percent of the black vote, and *that* was enough to propel him to victory in a historically non-Democratic state.

According to the Center for American Progress, in 2016, just 66 percent of eligible black women cast their ballots on Election Day, down from 74 percent in 2012 and 75 percent in 2008, greatly impacting the outcome of the election. Yet, black women's turnout in 2018 surged 16 percentage points from that of previous midterm elections, from 41 percent to 57 percent at a time when it was clear that change was needed under the Trump regime. A recent analysis from Groundswell and the AAPI (Asian Americans and Pacific Islanders) Civic Engagement Fund found that women of color fueled the massive increase in turnout nationwide by mobilizing friends and family and engaging voters beyond the ballot box. If 2008 or 2012 turnout levels were replicated in 2020, black women would cast at least 1 million more ballots than they did in 2016, reaching a total of roughly 11 million votes. Let me remind you that Donald Trump won the electoral college by a margin of 77,744 votes.

Progressives need to understand that unless you explicitly speak to black women and women of color, directly addressing the issues that impact us the most, you can't rely upon our support to win. Candidates need to start showing such support by investing campaign money where these demographics reside, showing that they believe in and support that constituency enough to put their money where their mouth is. And herein lies the problem. When Democrats think they have black and brown voters in the bag, they decide *not* to invest in those communities because they're considered a given, and the decision is made to invest campaign resources elsewhere. Risk-averse candidates prefer not to step out on a limb to invest in communities they've never invested in or spent time with before. Even if their previous strategies haven't been successful, they still tend to go with strategies they've always used, targeting voters they've always targeted. This is exactly the wrong strategy because it shows that the candidate would rather go down with the ship, stubbornly believing that they can win using their old methods, rather than listening to what communities of color have to say and what they need—even though, for Democratic candidates, it's these very communities that will get them elected.

Trust is earned, and Democrats have to earn the trust of voters before relying upon their support at the ballot box, just as Doug Jones did in Alabama. When politicians speak for people who don't necessarily have the power to speak up for themselves, that is when they are demonstrating what real leadership looks like. The best politicians are those who take the time to really listen to the people of color who represent the needs of our community, beyond just a cursory attempt at getting our support in the final weeks of a campaign by going to a couple of church services.

Democrats need to invest in a political infrastructure, consisting of money and boots on the ground, that puts black women at the forefront of policy. As activist Bree Newsome told me, the formula is pretty straightforward: "If you have black women organizing, mobilized, and you provide the infrastructure for them to turn out and to encourage their communities to turn out, that's how you win elections." But Democrats are traditionally too reluctant to put money into party infrastructure in places where they haven't traditionally won, but the future isn't going to look like the past. Politics is about relationships, and no candidate or political party can understand what specific communities need if they aren't engaging directly with the people who live in them. That means investing in building those relationships through time and in personnel tasked with maintaining constant communication. And that investment in on-the-ground personnel needs to focus on hiring black staff to engage with black people. If candidates don't have us working with them, they won't establish any real connection with the black community.

We need to build infrastructure in communities of color to educate and register voters and to ensure that they can cast their ballots—fighting the culture of voter suppression, which was done recently, during the 2018 midterms, in states like Georgia. Then, once the ballots are cast, everyone needs to roll up their sleeves because that's only phase one. When the candidate gets into office, we need to continue with this infrastructure and team strategy.

One of my favorite moments during the 2016 Hillary Clinton campaign came right at the beginning. Denise Horn decided that we needed to go to Black Girls Rock!, which is an annual special that BET (Black Entertainment Television) started with Beverly Bond to honor black women in entertainment, fashion, politics, and culture. The award ceremony was meant to create an intentional space to reward and honor black women specifically. Not women. *Black* women. There are so few spaces that actually do this, so putting Hillary in this space to just witness what was happening was really important. The black girl crew on the campaign decided that we needed to make a concerted effort in crafting the words that Hillary Clinton was going to speak to women like us. We wanted her message to be lasting, to be authentic.

The speech-writing team, while diverse with regards to gender, did not, at the time, have any black women on it. We knew that if Hillary was going to say something at this event about a black woman that she knew, like Maya Angelou, we needed to make sure that we had a verifiable picture proving Hillary Clinton was not just name-dropping. We knew that some were skeptical about a rich white lady showing up as a messenger of racial justice at an event honoring Rihanna, so we worked on her remarks with the head speechwriter, Dan Schwerin, knowing full well that any misstep could go viral. It was pretty funny to see Dan's face as the Black Girl Magic crew came marching into his office in formation to help craft the remarks. We pointed to areas in her remarks where Hillary could be her authentic self without seeming to be pandering. That's a difficult line to walk, but it was important for us to have Hillary speak directly to black women. And hiring staff who can make sure you understand communities of which you aren't a part is the key to appearing thoughtful and genuine—and *being* thoughtful and genuine.

Introducing the Black Girls Rock! founder Beverly Bond, Hillary said, "Black women are changemakers and path makers and ground shakers. My life has been changed by strong black women leaders, from Marian Wright Edelman to Dorothy Height to Maya Angelou. There are still a lot of barriers holding back African Americans and black women in particular, so a gathering like this, filled with so many powerful, strong women, is a rebuke to every single one of those barriers. All of our kids, no matter what zip code they live in, deserve a good teacher and a good school, a safe community, and clean water to drink."

I think that was and still is the right message because a white candidate like Hillary Clinton needed to demonstrate that she sees us, that she understands and can address the issues that leave so many families sick and tired of being sick and tired. It was a message that focused on what black families need from their government without hesitation. Too often Democrats wax poetic about the importance of the Midwest, without any mention of all of the black women who live in Detroit. And those women notice that omission. They want to know that they are seen. Hillary's very brief cameo was meant to signal and boost their achievements and to give a nod to the sisterhood.

We black women should be at the center of the campaign and the conversation since we are voting at higher rates than any other demographic and are impacting outcomes. I regret that we didn't duplicate this type of effort with black women day in and day out. The Black Girls Rock! Event was a one-time event. We didn't do enough, but that's not because the campaign didn't have the desire or make the effort to reach black women voters and speak directly to them. In my view, doing something to reflect that you respect the voice and views of the base of the party is only something that can be done through action. Words ring very hollow for communities that have for so long been promised consideration and a laundry list of policies only to be disappointed when their elected officials, once in office, mostly ignore them—and then disingenuously reengage them when their votes are needed again for reelection.

In hindsight, our message was challenged by media filters and wrongheaded assumptions about who Hillary Clinton was as a person and what she wanted to do for communities of color. Dammit, we tried. It just wasn't enough. Much of our efforts never reached the consciousness of an already Clinton-skeptical black America. Even during 2016, I remember coming in with lots of ideas for attracting black Millennials, and I recall people nodding fervently. But we never executed any of those ideas. And then, around three days into early voting, the campaign higher-ups suddenly said, "We need an emergency meeting. We need all of your ideas for black Millennials." At that point, I'd been working in the campaign for a year. All these ideas had already been discussed on the first day, the second day, the third day, the fourth day, and so on. We'd been talking about them the whole time, and the black Millennial vote shouldn't have been taken for granted. We shouldn't have taken anything for granted.

During the 2020 Democratic primaries, without a solid candidate race to unite them, black women's support has been splintered among several candidates. The candidates haven't known how to talk to black women. They don't know how to relate to us, us intersectional beings of at least two oppressed groups. But what eventual Democratic nominees need to keep in mind is that without the full backing of such a huge voting bloc, it will be that much harder for the Democratic candidate to win the presidential race of 2020. We did the best we could in 2016, but it's not going to cut it in the future.

If you're learning about Hillary Clinton's depth of black campaign talent for the first time, it's because the campaign lacked visibility from the outside. We should have pushed the press to do more profiles of the staff so American voters could see that people just like them were standing right there with Hillary and working with her to figure out the problems and the "solutions" that haven't worked in the past. I never questioned Hillary's commitment to black women because I was surrounded by reminders every day; she was completely aware and acknowledged that we were a critical component to achieving anything. I never questioned her understanding that black women would be the foundation of her own coalition for presidency. She saw what so many of the 2020 nominees for the Democratic primary nomination failed to see or simply ignored—that she needed black women on her side to be a successful and well-rounded nominee. I always say you can tell when candidates have black women on staff by the way they speak. They rarely misspeak when it comes to important issues of race and gender, and if they do misspeak, it's often because they didn't listen to those black women.

During this presidential election cycle, when there were several Democratic candidates of color, it was more import-ant than ever for that representation and experience to be reflected in the messaging and the perspectives behind the eventual nominee, particularly since the lone black woman who ran, Senator Kamala Harris, got pushed out of the race due to lagging poll numbers and stagnant fundraising. It's not to say that Harris shoulders no responsibility for any campaign missteps she made, like her slow response to criti-cisms of her record as a prosecutor. But statistically speaking, women have a harder time raising money in political cam-paigns, and for women of color, it's even more challenging to fundraise. That Harris was able to put up a credible effort is a testament to her strength as a candidate in a crowded field full of traditional white male options.

Hillary's campaign had more black women on staff than any other campaign in American history, and the black women I was surrounded by day in and day out were—simply put—magic. We had what you always want in a workplace—each other's backs. We backed each other up in meetings when sensitive issues like race and gender came up in discussions, a frequent theme in a campaign for a woman presidential candidate against Donald Trump, and we always reminded one another why we were there and whose perspectives we were representing. Though the 2020 race came down, once again, to septuagenarian white males, the future does provide a wide opening for female candidates and candidates of color who understand that their own lived experiences as non-white males are relevant to American policy and that their own authenticity will garner them the votes needed to impact that policy. The future face of power doesn't have to look like the white male presidents of the past. If you speak directly to the issues that people care about, they will be engaged in the way we need going forward, and no group is more important than black women whose political influence shapes entire households and, by extension, entire communities.

Democrats need to demonstrate that they understand the task at hand. The 2020 election is not about the 77,744 white votes that gave Donald Trump the electoral college; it's about the broader electorate that is younger, increasingly female, and incredibly diverse. There is always fear of a backlash to this type of messaging, but that doesn't mean we should cower in fear. America is evolving. Does the future of the Democratic Party look like a seventy-year-old white man? Or does it look like members of The Squad? Perhaps it looks like Senator Cory Booker or Secretary Julián Castro, who both entered the 2020 race vying for the same Democratic nomination as Biden. With the makeup of the electorate shifting so dramatically, why hasn't that also changed the makeup of those we choose to put into positions of power? It's a huge problem that the Democratic electorate is becoming increasingly diverse, and yet the candidates at the top of our choices for president don't reflect that diversity.

In a leaked strategy memo, 2018 Georgia gubernatorial candidate Stacey Abrams said that Democrats need to let go of the past and look to the voters of the future. To her credit as mentioned, she was able to effectively duplicate an Obama coalition in Georgia by bringing new voters into the democratic process. Abrams wrote in *The Abrams Playbook: The Strategy and Path to Victory in 2020*:

My campaign for governor engaged, organized, and in-spired traditional voters and brought new voices to the table. Although I am not Georgia's governor, our unprec-edented campaign received more votes than any Demo-cratic candidate for any office in Georgia history, fueled by record-breaking support from white voters and pres-idential-level turnout and support from the diverse com-munities of color in our state. However, I am not the only candidate who can create a coalition and a strategy to win . . . and Georgia is not the only state poised to take advan-tage of demographic changes.

What Abrams understands is that the next moment in American politics is an opportunity of a lifetime, and Obama's coalition of voters is still the key to Democrats winning elec-tions in the future. As Abrams noted: "We do not lose win-nable white voters because we engage communities of color. We do not lose urban votes because we campaign in rural areas." You simply have to tailor your messaging accordingly.

The ever-growing mistrust between communities of color and the Democratic establishment is the result of poor efforts. Everything boils down to issues of identity. We haven't fully acknowledged the fact that the foundation of this country originated in racism. Although our founding documents cite freedom and justice for all, anyone who isn't white knows that promise doesn't apply universally to everyone. In this coun-try, a person's skin color dictates their treatment, and when they aren't white, historically that means they aren't treated as well as someone who is white. Once we acknowledge that and, accordingly, change the politics and allow our govern-ments to be more representative, we can simultaneously start to change the culture. If we are finally going to start living up to the vision of a powerful multiracial country that represents all communities, we have to give the government back to the people. Once this newly formed and even more diverse coalition recognizes their newfound power, they can and will effectively elect candidates who actually represent and reflect their interests and values. This may not look like an old white man standing in the Oval Office any longer, and the Democrats must learn to not only be OK with that fact but to welcome it.

It's time to adopt a future where our leaders understand what it's truly like for people to live paycheck to paycheck, what it's truly like for *all* of America's citizens to live their day-to-day existences. If you don't have people in power who know what it's like to have a sick parent in need of long-term care, then you don't have people with the right perspectives on health care policy. If you don't have people in power who know what it's like to have to spend your entire salary on childcare, then you don't have people with the right perspectives on how class and education intersect either. That basic empathy is essential in the future of legislating, and we've gotten so far away from that in recent decades. Now's the time to bring that focus and that voice back to this country, with black women at the center of the messaging and seated prominently at the table.

CHAPTER 6

The Hashtag
Kids

CLOSE YOUR EYES and picture a Millennial in your head. You know Millennials: they're the generation that has spawned a million articles about their work ethic, their attitudes, and their propensity to still live at home after the Great Recession got them off to adulthood with a bad start.

But be honest with yourself: Did you picture an eighteen-year-old college student? Would it surprise you to learn that the oldest Millennials are now almost forty years old? The Millennial generation and Generation Z coming up behind us (the folks who are going to be age eighteen to twenty-three in 2020) are, collectively, more progressive than the generations that came before us. We are also more culturally diverse and supportive of expanding equal rights and freedoms to everyone, holding the values of equality for everyone, protections for the LBGTQ+ community, and reproductive health care access as central components to our political belief system. This generational difference, compared to our parents and grandparents, has created a remarkable mix of perspectives in the upcoming election, but bridging this generational divide can be helpful in understanding the voting preferences to date and what voters may want to hear in the future. To put it simply: the teenaged Beyoncé who was in Destiny's Child now has a different set of political needs and expectations than the thirty-eight-year-old Millennial Beyoncé who is mother to Blue Ivy and the twins.

We've finally reached a moment in time where the young folks will have their say, where they now have the numbers to become a political force for good. According to Pew, there are about 75 million eligible voters that are in the Baby Boomer generation, born between 1944 and 1964. In 2016, Boomers made up 31 percent of eligible voters and Millennials tracked closely behind, making up 26 percent of the electorate. But in the most recent election, 2018, Millennials and Gen Z outvoted the older generations in the midterms. The young folk are now speaking up and speaking out.

Millennials and Generation Z are less likely to identify with a political party, but they are more likely than previous generations to vote in the upcoming elections, and they are motivated by the actual *issues* that impact them daily as opposed to being motivated by the personalities of particular politicians. Seventy-seven percent of the respondents to an election study done by *Teen Vogue* magazine and Ipsos, a global market and research firm, said they were definitely going to vote in the 2020 election. In this poll given to readers aged eighteen to thirty-four, the "top three most important issues for American political leaders to address were noted as health care, the economy, and education, even if those polled disagree on the specific policy proposals that best address those issues." These generations get how this works. They understand that if you want different policies, policies that speak to our lived experiences, then you need to vote for those who understand those lived experiences, not just for a TV personality you may like. It's not rocket science.

This generation also keenly understands that the lack of movement on crucial issues in American society, like the climate crisis, is the result of the elected officials who we've put in power. According to 73 percent of *Teen Vogue* respondents, our future is at risk because of climate change, and 69 percent say the government won't act quickly enough to stop it. Seventy-two percent support providing government subsidies to clean energy providers, and 66 percent support placing a tax on carbon pollution. Millennials and Generation Z know that time is running out, and that there isn't time to wait for the older generation of veteran politicians to make a move *for* us.

It's no question that culture shapes political outcomes, and this new generation is focused on making sure that rights are expanded and not infringed upon. The connectivity of this generation through social media platforms and the internet has made it much harder for these young people to ignore the marginalized and to discriminate against those who come from different backgrounds than they do. They are exposed to a barrage of information on a daily—even hourly—basis via their cell phone and technological devices, which most carry with them at all times. That has created a progressive and engaged generation of activist-minded voters.

It's no longer controversial to say that social media is the conduit or medium for the world. The internet and social media generation gets a lot of flak for its so-called hashtag activism, but it's these same hashtag movements that have pushed public policy into the homes and everyday conversations of Americans, igniting change and functioning as an echo chamber for a revolutionary call for justice, diversity, and progressivism. In the civil rights era of the 1960s, marches and sit-ins were the popular form of mass protest. Today, mass protest also happens through hashtag organizing. The paper flyers that organized the Montgomery bus boycott would've looked like this today: #MontgomeryBoycott. Yet, the goal is the same.

Today, organizing and activism mostly happen online. It can be as simple as changing your avatar to a color that signals solidarity with a cause, signing digital petitions, or organizing online collective boycotts. One such example is the recent boycotting of campaign contributions from the Koch brothers and their affiliates. Don't like that the Koch brothers finance politicians who block an expansion of worker protections? Then don't buy Brawny paper towels. That's the work Color Of Change, a progressive nonprofit civil rights advocacy organization. They successfully pressured companies to do right by workers, by starting a social media movement. Social media activism can often help achieve more than some politicians. When politicians take financial contributions from big corporations, they're more likely to end up in their pocket, making policy decisions to benefit their benefactors, which, in turn, keeps their contributions rolling in, rather than making policy decisions to benefit their constituents. Politicians who receive contributions from the Koch brothers aren't going to push for reformist legislation that tackles climate change and promotes clean energy because that would threaten the profits of Koch Industries.

Now, imagine Congress filled with legislators who are funded by companies that make money from oil, gas, and coal. They have an incentive to maintain the status quo and continue making billions of dollars in profit while the climate crisis looms just over the horizon. Or think about the two largest for-profit prison companies, GEO Group and Corrections Corporation of America, who spend millions of dollars on lobbying and campaign contributions to support policies that keep people behind bars, overwhelmingly young people of color. Then think about the impact these corporations have on black and brown communities, which are fighting for criminal justice reform. The money is fueling policy action and inaction. But that's where social media intersects with the real world as a tool to empower people all over the globe to mobilize for change on our own rather than waiting for self-serving politicians to do it for us.

Millennial's hashtags and digital organizing are sometimes criticized by the civil rights generation of our parents because the "work" isn't as visible. We can see the black-and-white photographs of Martin Luther King Jr. and Congressman John Lewis marching and putting their bodies on the line, but we don't see the stills of the many behind-the-scenes meetings that organized those marches. Likewise, the marches of today's generation are the result of countless hours of organizing online. With Black Lives Matter and Ferguson in the Obama era as precursors to a new era of political protest and activism, Millennials and Generation Z don't wait for permission to enact change.

The Millennial generation has grown up with the internet and social media for a large chunk of our lives—Generation Z for even longer than us. We're techno-savvy and have shown how we can use social media to shape and change entire ideologies and outlooks on old problems that needed to be seen through a modern lens. It's unlikely that criminal justice issues would have come front and center in the 2020 presidential campaigns without the hashtag #BlackLivesMatter, a social justice movement created by three black women. In previous election cycles, the police killings of black people didn't make it to the twenty-four-hour news cycle. Twitter didn't even exist in the 2004 election cycle and was rarely utilized in 2008 beyond what folks were having for lunch. So, 2012 and beyond is when hashtag activism as we know it was born and took root in American culture and politics.

During the 1990s, the Democratic establishment was reluctant to publicly discuss racism, and the Clinton era implemented "tough on crime" policies and a crime bill that criminalized youth of color and incarcerated an entire generation of black and brown men. Hence, the moment in Bill Clinton's presidency that became a euphemism for this resistance to honest race discussion: the Sister Souljah moment. These moments happen when a politician publicly disavows an extremist group, ideology, or person who is perceived to have some connection with said politician's political party. This phenomenon was even covered by Bret Stephens, a *New York Times* opinion columnist, who commented that "the point of a Sister Souljah moment isn't to ingratiate a candidate to the party base. It's to demonstrate independence and nerve. And furnish evidence that the candidate is of the center, not the fringe." Of the center—imagine that.

The original Sister Souljah moment happened in a 1992 *Washington Post* interview where the political activist, author, and MC spoke out against the violence of the Los Angeles riots. Yet, police brutality and killings continued into an era where social media could be used as a tool to amplify and combat these injustices, such as when political activism went viral via the hashtag #BlackLivesMatter after the 2013 killing of Trayvon Martin, a seventeen-year-old African American boy in Florida. Martin was walking home with a benign pack of Skittles and an iced tea when neighborhood watch cop George Zimmerman antagonized, shot, and killed him.

Alicia Garza, Opal Tometi, and Patrisse Cullors (the latter two are of the Millennial generation) created the hashtag that sparked a real social justice movement. The tragedy caused national unrest and forced the conversation toward racial justice issues, which became a matter of everyday concern in the mainstream. President Obama said in a public statement that "Trayvon could have been my son," marking a moment in history when the United States government seemed poised to respond to the violence and racial disparities that too many generations of black and brown Americans have had to endure on their own.

Social media, through #MeToo, has amplified the conversation around sexual harassment and pushed the Democratic Party and the nation closer to a reality where we can be free from harassment in the workplace and in public. What's clear now is that this generational disconnect is not just by way of technology and gadgets, but it's also in the way we approach the public policy that governs our lives. We need to utilize these tools to reform the Democratic coalition, to rally voters, and to embrace members of younger generations of Democrats who are even now vying to effect change.

The #MeToo movement has also rocked the world and turned "accountability" into something that's finally talked about in mainstream culture. The framework for understanding rape culture has shifted. Grassroots movements via social media are growing every day and allow us to reach millions with one unified message—stop sexual harassment and violence against women—with the simple tap of a button on our phones. These messages can now effectively reach our lawmakers in real time.

The term *Millennial* was coined when the median-aged of this generation were barely out of high school—well over a decade ago—and exploded onto the mainstream in a trend that has yet to die down. Millennials have wrongly been framed as a bunch of "kids," eliciting nostalgic images of marijuana-loving teens and fresh-out-of-college hipsters, even though that's not necessarily who we are anymore. This is an inadequate label, often powered by older generations—a label that is out of touch and out of date and meant to minimize our voices in a "there, there, children" sort of way. That misunderstanding allows for this generation's serious concerns to be sidelined by the formerly more consistent voting blocs of older demographics. But our generation's voter numbers have increased, outnumbering those of older generations. And now, *we* demand to be heard. As discussed, Millennials are *now* a generation of people that includes those of us who are nearly forty years old. So, the "kid" narrative is well past its prime and ripe for debunking. Millennials are no longer a generation of college kids, and our policy concerns aren't only about student loans and legalizing marijuana.

There will always be a new group of young voters coming of age to cast their ballots, but the Millennial generation is currently at the forefront of intersecting political issues and social change movements that go beyond what conventional partisan framing has supported and promoted in the past. We don't know what an election outcome looks like if 77 percent of Americans under the age of forty show up to vote, as the *Teen Vogue*/Ipsos Survey indicated. That kind of turnout and infusion of progressive worldviews could radically change the makeup of all levels of government. We normally discuss the youth vote as if it's a stagnant, unchanging group of people who are always trying to find colleges with affordable tuition. But today's voters under forty are trying to purchase homes after paying down crippling student loan debt they racked up during school, only to graduate into the biggest economic downturn in American history. This generation graduated out of college and into adulthood directly into the Great Recession and its aftermath, denied the economic reliability and stability that previous generations have enjoyed, which helped them to plant their roots and grow.

Business Insider reported that the financial crisis created a domino effect of damage to the economic security of an entire generation. It put us behind previous generations and kept us in a perpetual spiral of near poverty as we struggled to pay the bills and pay for everyday needs like housing and food. With everything falling apart around us, Millennials struggled through stagnant wage growth and exponential increases in the cost of living to evolve away from the paycheck-to-paycheck status quo norm in a never-ending push toward middle-classdom and the upper end of the economic graph. The older Millennials have been tagged as a "lost generation," where wealth accumulation is out of reach and saving for any kind of retirement seems like an unrealistic pipe dream. "The Great Recession has divided millennials into two distinct groups—those who took the greatest hit from the recession and dealt with a tough job market, and those who experienced the recovery period, entering a better job market. In a nutshell, the oldest millennials went through the eye of the storm, while the youngest millennials caught the tailwind. . . . Older millennials are still recovering from the recession." We have to ask ourselves: Is this area of our lives being adequately represented in our public policy? And if not, shouldn't it be?

Understanding the full scope of concerns young people have and how they may differ from older voters is the first step of engagement and, hopefully, activation. This is why Democrats must continue to embrace the concerns of new generations of voters—to help the party engage more voters, keeping the Democratic Party machine churning and moving forward progressively, as Barack Obama did to create his Obama coalition in 2008 and 2012. If the 2018 midterms are instructive for the power of this movement, then the future is going to look more like Alexandria Ocasio-Cortez and a lot less like Mitch McConnell in both style and substance. Understanding that Millennials are now full-grown adults who harness enormous voting power is the first step toward progress, and then understanding that we are focused on issues previous generations ignored or failed to adequately address—like climate change, Medicare for All, and police brutality—means we have a greater sense of urgency because we are the ones who now have to live with the consequences of inaction.

Millennials are currently the largest and most diverse generation in the United States. Our size and diversity are what allow our political power. We aren't a one-size-fits-all generation, and we aren't looking for a one-size-fits-all party or candidate. According to the *Teen Vogue*/Ipsos Survey on what young people want: "If younger voters like those we surveyed agree that the climate crisis is a threat, if they see student debt as a hindrance to their lives, and view government-provided health care as a potential good, then that has big implications for both major political parties, and the entire population." That Millennials and Generation Z are more liberal leaning than previous generations means Democrats can attract these new and passionate young voters to engage for the long term.

Numbers have power in politics, and it's our numbers that need to be respected and heard as we mobilize toward modern-day issues that impact our society. The next generation behind Millennials, Generation Z are going to make up 10 percent of the 2020 electorate. Just to make the math clear: in 2020, less than a quarter of the electorate (23 percent) will be aged sixty-five and older, so the older Baby Boomers and members of the Silent Generation will have less of a say in shaping election outcomes than they've had in the past. However, many of our policy concerns do cross over with theirs. That means that issues like Medicare for All, which 59 percent of the *Teen Vogue* survey respondents said was a policy they looked for in a presidential candidate, is a platform that can unify the generations of voters and motivate them to cast their ballots.

In addition to being the most diverse (48 percent nonwhite), Millennials are also projected to be the best-educated generation yet, which means the messaging the party uses to attract these votes needs to account for this diversity of perspectives and the disparity in ages from the current old guard. In 2020, 55 percent of Generation Z voters will be white and 45 percent will be nonwhite. By comparison, Baby Boomer voters are nearly 75 percent white. This shift in the demographic (from 75 percent white to 55 percent white) means that people of color now have a more collective voice than ever before, a message that Democrats need to see and understand. The makeup of who is voting for candidates is becoming *less* white, transforming the representation we should see in our leaders today as well as what issues are centered as important to this nation. This shift in the makeup of who is voting for candidates will transform the representation in progressive politics.

Just as these voter demographics are changing, the younger generations' use of social media makes Millennials and Gen Zers a force to be reckoned with at the ballot box. Take the Parkland survivors, for example—those powerful voices you've heard coming from your screens and punching through on your social media ever since the tragic high school massacre on Valentine's Day, 2018. They've taken on gun reform with a vigor that is wholly absent in today's Democratic Party. Immediately after the Parkland shooting, the country responded as we always do in the face of unexpected tragedy—thoughts and prayers extended, tearful vigils, but no real action taken to bring justice to this heinous crime and to change matters for the next potential victims of gun violence.

The Parkland students and march organizers, including Emma Gonzales and David Hogg, organized with youth activists in Chicago and across the country to build the biggest march in Washington, DC, in American history: March for Our Lives. What the Parklanders understand is that being a member of Congress is not a lifetime appointment. We can vote them out. Although some of the bigger names—like Senator Marco Rubio, who took millions in donations from the NRA and who never votes to support expanding background checks or other forms of gun safety legislation—haven't yet been impacted by their activism. The Parklanders directly confronting any legislators who take NRA blood money is the start of a trend.

These young activists have clearly organized around a political issue that is important to them. Mass shooting after mass shooting is evidence that something is broken in our American political system. These Parkland activists understand that we have the collective power to enact change, and they've already mobilized it.

March for Our Lives was so large, diverse, and impact-ful because youth voter registration increased by 41 percent after the Parkland massacre. There is normally a huge gap in turnout between older and younger voters at all levels of government, from local elections up through the presidential level, but after Parkland, these young activists started mobi-lizing around state laws and voter registration. After Park-land things were different. The Parkland leaders understood that to effect change, they have to vote. At the March for Our Lives, co-organizer Gonzalez said, "Fight for your lives before it's someone else's job." The direct link between voting and political power allowed the Parkland students to be a force for good and to demand attention from all of the powers that be from the outset.

The strength of their movement is bred from two essential truths: first, that guns are an issue impacting people of all races and class levels in all communities, and second, that in order to fight special interest groups, you must organize an intersectional movement with the power to impact lives long term. This young generation of activists didn't just stand around waiting for the status quo to change on its own. They equipped themselves with knowledge and manpower and fought for the change they knew they needed to see in the nation. The elected leaders at all levels suddenly had to do something about guns—and quickly. They created one mas-sive movement that simply could not be ignored.

One year after the Parkland shooting, eight states, in-cluding Florida, passed red flag laws, which allow family members to ask law enforcement to temporarily restrict an individual's access to a gun if that person poses a danger to him- or herself or to others. Eleven states have passed laws that make it more difficult for a domestic abuser to get a gun. They weren't successful in defeating Ron DeSantis, a 2018 Republican candidate with an A-plus rating from the National Rifle Association who managed to get elected to office as governor of Florida. However, their efforts to register and mobilize young people to the polls, often voting for the first time, created voters who are more likely to vote in the next election—and the one after that. In many ways, this movement normalized political participation for young people as something the cool kids are doing—though the issues at stake are anything but childish.

Whether we're trying to solve gun violence, racial injustice, sexual harassment, or health care inequities, we must organize across the intersection of class and race, engaging every single type of person who is touched by the issue. These Parkland activists did just that. In the past, we either organized around preventing inner city violence or we worked in suburban areas to prevent mass shootings, but we rarely brought the two groups together. This generation changed that. Their coalition platforms—both on social media and beyond—are based on the very thing that can propel all Democratic policy forward. Their platforms are built on identity-based politics as gun violence survivors.

The Parklanders understand the unwillingness of the Republican Party to compromise on issues of gun laws and historical white supremacy, and they realize that trying to find compromise in the middle is a futile endeavor indeed—common ground with Republicans isn't always the ground our progressive movement or Democratic Party should be standing on. Bree Newsome put it best when she told me why moderates like Joe Biden aren't gaining the support of young people:

I don't need you [Biden] to work with Republicans. I need you to push the Republicans out and I need you to vigorously fight for an agenda that will actually do something for me, because working with the Republicans means you're working with people who are trying to destroy my ability to thrive. . . . You're talking about working with the people who are trying to take away my health care, with the people who make these sexist and racist remarks all the time, the people who are basically responsible for all this gun violence . . . when you think about the issues that are at the forefront, particularly in the black community, and working people . . . the Republican agenda is the opposite.

A moderate approach to guns won't solve the issue of gun violence in America, and the way out isn't by playing nice with a Republican Party indebted to the National Rifle Association. What we need is to continue the wave of new kids on the congressional block, that diverse coalition of Democrats who won election in the blue wave of 2018 midterms, who are bringing fresh eyes to these intractable problems. They aren't looking to be loyal to parties simply for the sake of doing so, as older generations have. This aggressive evolution allows the Democratic Party to recognize and remold itself into the image of the party's younger, more diverse, and more progressive contemporary base.

But social media, of course, isn't only for the young. It's also a forum where you can see the clash between the old guard and the new playing out in real time, as we saw with Donald Trump's offensive and bigoted tweet in the summer of 2019 about The Squad: Representatives Alexandria Ocasio-Cortez (nicknamed AOC), Ilhan Omar, Rashida Talib, and Ayanna Pressley—all young women of color who are known for their outspoken candor on public policy for creating a collective following of nearly ten million on Twitter. On the surface, this seemed like it was just another xenophobic attack launched from the president's Twitter account, just another in a long line of racially based online assaults from our commander in chief. But this particular tweet also represented a generational disconnect and a growing fear of the new and more progressive women of color who are running and winning elections.

The Squad are all firsts—three were under the age of forty when they won their elections. AOC is the youngest woman ever elected to Congress at the age of twenty-nine. Pressley is the first black person elected to Congress from the state of Massachusetts, and Omar and Talib are the first female Muslim members of Congress, ever. They were dubbed The Squad because of an unscheduled photo shoot during congressional orientation during which AOC used the hashtag #SquadGoals in the caption of the photo posted on social media. The nickname stuck. Then one summer day, Trump decided to tweet out that The Squad should "go back" to the countries they came from, and the name became a moniker used by the national media. This idea that we should "send her back" is truly the most virulent strain of American racism and white supremacy. Never mind the fact that the only foreign-born congresswoman in The Squad is Ilhan Omar, who came here to the United States with her family as a Somalian refugee at age ten. Ayanna Pressley was born in Cincinnati; Ocasio-Cortez was born in the Bronx; and Rashida Talib was born in Detroit.

His xenophobia was clear: the message was that these women of color weren't American—certainly not "American" enough for his base. It was a rare moment where the mainstream media did not hesitate to label his tweets racist because telling these four women of color to go back to their country is based on the premise that only white people can be "true" Americans and citizens. But the moment also revealed that white establishment Democrats have either a blind spot or a complete disregard for defending these kinds of attacks right when they happen. The delay in response from older members of the Democratic guard appeared to be a moment of dispute. The Democratic Party has to be united and understand that the new generation will be more visible and more diverse, which makes them more obvious targets for attacks from Trump and the opposition. The initial reluctance of Democratic leadership to stand up against Trump's attacks revealed a divide between the generations of elected Democrats, and there is no group more representative of how the next generation of leadership will look than The Squad.

Just as our generation has learned to harness social media as a means to effect progressivism and positive change, Donald Trump understands the power of social media, too. He uses it as a weapon to align his movement against shared enemies. He tweets almost every single morning to seventy million loyal followers who connect with him and feel that his use of social media makes him one of them. He uses social media to pass on a simple message of us against them. He throws out childish nicknames for his rivals, like "Crooked Hillary," "Liddle Marco Rubio," and "Mini Mike Bloomberg." Despite this power, Trump's Twitter feed is characterized by resentment and pettiness typical of the kind of drama you would see on the finale of your favorite *Real Housewives* season, not what we should expect from the person who holds the highest office in our country, our commander in chief. In Trump's eyes, you are either with him and his supporters or you are the enemy, one of "them"—the left-wing media, liberals, Democrats, people of color. While Trump understands how to weaponize social media as a tool for division, the younger generations of activists understand that it can also be a tool for bringing people together around a common political or social cause. It can be used to create our *own* movements.

Social media makes these generational gaps and policy disputes all the more visible, allowing us immediate access to information from the convenience of our phones and electronics, and visibility shows us firsthand how The Squad's outspoken public personas are a direct threat to the status quo. Their unapologetically liberal positioning in a party grappling with the coming shifts is a risk to the traditional power centers. They don't just look different from the leaders we are so used to seeing in positions of political power; they also wield their ideologies in a fundamentally dissimilar way. It's the combination of their youth, gender, ethnicities, and outspoken entry into the 116th Congress that have made them such lightning rods of controversy. They represent the future and the very electorate that is now strong enough to push back against the powers that traditionally centered anybody but us. And the use of social media by this generation is making that all the more possible.

The refocus of policy discussions on issues that women of color, like The Squad, care the most about will upend the entire establishment, but it will push the party toward policies that will include the whole of our democracy, not just the few. If the president is afraid of four freshman congresswomen who represent the voices of millions of new and future voters, then there is a real reason to be afraid—and social media exposed his fears. It's not just an illusion that those who have historically been in positions of power have now responded to this generational shift in leadership so fearfully and so palpably.

The Squad is an example of what is possible for the progressive movement going forward, and they wear their strength and vibrancy like rightful badges of honor for all to see on their social media platforms. When the right-wing media goes after AOC for a perceived misstep, like wearing an expensive dress on ABC's *The View*, she claps back immediately and in a language young people understand. She speaks internet. The Squad is the embodiment of what is possible in the next generation of American political influence, with sharp moral clarity and the ability to punch up at the people in power to speak on behalf of those without enough political muscle to be heard. Those communities have long gone ignored, yet the same party leaders continue to show up in the election cycles. Well, now it's time for them to pay up, and social media—wielded by this emerging generation of leaders—will be the new way of ensuring accountability.

Just look at the priorities that The Squad members have focused on in their very first terms in Congress. AOC has focused on a six-bill package called A Just Society, which includes policies targeting poverty, affordable housing, and climate change. "Representative Ocasio-Cortez believes that we must build a just society to protect our communities and uplift our neighbors. A Just Society legislation aims to combat one of the greatest threats to our country, our democracy, and our freedom: economic inequality." AOC believes that no one should be too poor to live. Living means housing. Living means food on the table. Living means health care for your family and not having to choose between that and other necessities. Describing her package, AOC said, "A Just Society aims to ensure that we are on a path towards shared prosperity for all. A just society provides a living wage, safe working conditions, and health care. A just society acknowledges the value of immigrants to our communities. A just society guarantees safe, comfortable, and affordable housing. By strengthening our social and economic foundations, we are preparing ourselves to embark on the journey to save our planet by rebuilding our economy and cultivating a just society."

Among the first bills that Representative Ilhan Omar, another Squad member, introduced to Congress was one focused on America's foreign policy role abroad, which too often results in the deaths of brown people in the Middle East and overly sanctioned communities riddled by conflicts predating the living generations. These newly minted members of Congress speak on behalf of the people who elected them, a diverse constituency that reflects the electorate America will grow into by 2045. The members of The Squad are an early symbol of this shift, and the right-wing backlash against them is evidence of their power and potential.

The shift in the power dynamic of who is represented in politics is something that resonates with voters under forty. These crucial lifeblood members infuse the next generation's energy and vision into the Democratic Party, and it is this next generation that now has the opportunity to legislate from the point of view of the masses' true, lived, experiences. Our culture, powered by social media sharing, is getting an education in what inclusion really means and looks like. We're understanding that representation really matters, and Millennials and Generation Z are powering and spreading this movement with their Twitter fingers and hashtag activism. That inclusive new era starts with making sure that no room, anywhere, is made up of only white people, and when it is, asking why and demanding immediate changes. The Squad are all history-making firsts, but they won't be the last of this type of authentic leaders of the current generation. They truly know how to connect with people and call out injustice with a level of clarity that requires everyone to stop and pay attention.

In many ways, I feel connected to the members of The Squad because we all have some lived experiences that overlap. Alexandria Ocasio-Cortez grew up in a predominantly white suburb outside New York City, and she attended Boston University. I grew up in Millburn, New Jersey, a predominantly white suburb outside New York City, and I attended Tufts University, right outside Boston. We're less than ten years apart in age. Navigating spaces that are majority white as a woman of color is unique. You are both hypervisible and completely invisible. You aren't assumed to be in the correct place at any given time; you might be accused of stealing things that go missing from dorm common areas. All eyes stare in your direction when the topic of race predictably comes up during collegiate discussions. Surviving this environment and coming out on the other side without a flicker of imposter syndrome is a feat in and of itself, and from my vantage point, AOC has at least shaken off a lot of those same fears that I feel inside myself. It's these connected lived experiences that we need to embrace in the Democratic Party. When I look at The Squad and these fresh, new members of

Congress and hear them speak, they sound like I would if I were a member of Congress; they care about the issues that I would press to change if I were in their shoes. They don't look like the faces of our government who have been in place for generations but don't look like nor resemble my lived experiences in any way. Instead, they resemble the whitewashed history of America currently battling to maintain their hundreds of years of power.

I don't normally hear myself in the experiences of Speaker Nancy Pelosi or Senator Chuck Schumer, but when AOC claps back at Republicans trolling her on Twitter with lyrics to a Cardi B song, she's speaking my language. She also can do this in a much more authentic way than, say, Hillary Clinton when she is name-dropping Beyoncé. It's this display of authenticity that allows the younger generation to connect with these new leaders and to finally get excited about engaging in American politics and our elections. Understandably, it takes years to build the list of contacts and political battle experiences that a leader like Pelosi has amassed, but it's this connection to the community and authenticity that's so important to young voters and that can get lost in translation with older politicians.

That adjustment in the lens through which we even imagine what's possible reflects a new paradigm for our politics. For far too long, we've had people in positions of power who were reluctant—if not outright resistant—to making the necessary changes to our legislature that would make America more equitable for everyone in everything from education to health care and beyond. They benefit from the status quo, and the people who look like them benefit from the status quo. Any radical changes threaten to upend America as we have come to know it, but for marginalized communities, the shift can't come soon enough. The current moment is evidence of just how big the threat is to the traditional white-powered politics that America has played since its founding, and this new wave of Twitter-wielding, hashtag-breeding American trailblazers has created a virtual battlefield on which to fight their battles just as effectively as they have raised the voice of the people and altered the modern-day ballot-box dynamics.

If the Millennials and Gen Zers combine their outsized share of the political power and then turn out to vote in 2020, it will be a moment when the entire political establishment will be forced to reckon with demographic realities. The way to make change starts with going out and talking to people about politics until they understand how every aspect of politics is personal. Now, technology allows us to get engaged like never before, using social platforms to get the message out, which can mobilize the vote. But it starts with speaking to our personal circles of influence, making sure everyone we know and love is registered (iwillvote.com is a great place to start). And, for those who want to push the needle even further than their one vote, they volunteer for the campaigns themselves.

Society should no longer pretend that the elections we've lived through before can predict the future. The country doesn't look like it did a generation ago, and that is a good thing, but our legislature shouldn't look the same way it did a generation ago either. We shouldn't fear this change, and we should embrace the young disruptors in Congress, both present and future, because they can help close the generational gap in diverse representation. From picket lines to the popular use of smartphones, American politics has seen a radical transformation in the methods and tools of communication. A greater sense of access to the people in positions of power in media and policy making allows for a two-way conversation as the voices of the historically marginalized who now have their hands wrapped around the media megaphone via the power of social media. This generational divide in American politics has been made wider and swifter than that of previous generations because of the gaping rift that the immediacy of modern-day technology has created. With this rapid shift in how we live our daily lives, how we consume our information, and how we interact with new ideas, a new trend of wokeness has swept the nation, creating two distinct camps: those who are and those who aren't.

Wokeness is not just about being aware of those other human beings living on this planet with full lives, backgrounds, and experiences. When the older generation or the established media types criticize young people for being woke, what they are really saying is that it's somehow a negative thing to have a high level of consciousness around issues of cultural injustice. But if you're a person of color, this wokeness is already historically in your blood. And though there exists a generational gap between today's hashtag kids of political change and previous generations' changemakers via organized protests and marches, we share that same urge to spread the message of the woke, and we must understand that we Democrats are all standing on the same side though our methods may be different. We haven't forgotten the importance of marching and how it paved the way for our movements today. Those past movements are still in our blood, just like the road to Selma is in my blood.

On the fiftieth anniversary of Bloody Sunday, I accompanied President Obama on Air Force One to Selma, Alabama, for a special annual march. I couldn't help but think about my aunt Janet and my own family's connection to that piece of history, so I called her the night before the trip from the back of the Bolt Bus to DC, and she told me about the journey she took to the march with my grandfather, Elmer Williams, when she was only a teenager.

She recounted how she hid from the Ku Klux Klan in a pickup truck her first night in Selma. There were rumors throughout the city that the Ku Klux Klan was looking for marchers to murder. When a group of them drove by my aunt and the church group led by my grandfather, she thought she was going to die.

Fifty years after my aunt hid in that truck, I was sitting on Air Force One, going to Selma under completely different circumstances and conditions with the first black president, Barack Obama. The group of journalists traveling with the president were all black: Charles Blow, Dwayne English, April Ryan, Rembert Browne, and me. The history of the moment deeply impacted all of us, but there was also a fun, family reunion vibe on Air Force One. Everyone was simply basking in the moment. During the president's remarks, I couldn't help but think of Aunt Janet. It truly felt like a joyous moment of American racial progress and a sign of a more equitable future. We had come such a long way from the brutality that took place on the Edmund Pettus Bridge five decades earlier.

It was at the foot of the Edmund Pettus Bridge that images of peaceful marchers being beaten by police on their protest from Selma to Montgomery were broadcast around the world.

Congressman John Lewis, who was nineteen at the time, was severely beaten and received a concussion and several other injuries. The juxtaposition between the peaceful protest and the police brutality forced President Lyndon Johnson down a pathway toward civil rights progress. That history lingered in the air when we watched America's first black president reflect on the bravery of those who marched with Dr. King on that day and also the two subsequent marches, including the one my family participated in. The moment was filled with both hope and promise as Lewis sat behind the president, looking into the crowd. President Obama couldn't have known what was to come in the next election, but his words that day are even more prescient now as America struggles through a demographic revolution:

> We do a disservice to the cause of justice by intimating that bias and discrimination are immutable, or that racial division is inherent to America. If you think nothing's changed in the past fifty years, ask somebody who lived through the Selma or Chicago or L.A. of the Fifties. Ask the female CEO who once might have been assigned to the secretarial pool if nothing's changed. Ask your gay friend if it's easier to be out and proud in America now than it was thirty years ago. To deny this progress—our progress—would be to rob us of our own agency; our responsibility to do what we can to make America better.

Of course, a more common mistake is to suggest that racism is banished, that the work that drew men and women to Selma is complete, and that whatever racial tensions remain are a consequence of those seeking to play the "race card" for their own purposes. We don't need political pundits to know that's not true. We just need to open our eyes and ears and hearts to know that this nation's racial history still casts its long shadow upon us. We know the march is not yet over, the race is not yet won, and that reaching that blessed destination where we are judged by the content of our character requires admitting as much. Our generation understands this just as much as previous generations did. The way we make our voices heard looks different now, but the change we're fighting for is still the same,and our strength is built on the backs of the work of the generations that came before us.

CHAPTER 7

The Blue Wave
Is Not
Uncle Joe

PICTURE IT: It's 1973 and the thirty-year-old Joseph R. Biden, full of youth and vim, is addressing a crowd at the City Club of Cleveland. He's just landed his Delaware Senate seat. Racist Strom Thurmond is still serving as South Carolina's senior senator. Alabama governor George Wallace switched his segregationist positions just the year prior. And it's just five years after the assassination of Reverend Dr. Martin Luther King Jr.

Joe Biden opens his mouth to address the crowd and what tumbles out is that "the two-party system . . . is good for the South and good for the Negro, good for the black in the South." He warns Democrats about attacking Republicans on Watergate, noting that "clearly Democrats are as immoral as Republicans, and maybe in big cities, a good deal more immoral in the traditional sense." And so started what would be a long history of a questionable understanding of his black constituency with words that are clearly incongruent with what he claims are his current political stances—words that would come back to haunt him during his bid for the Democratic nomination.

Just two years later, Biden is on record questioning the very concept of institutionalized racism, according to a *Washington Post* article. More than questioning it, he categorically *denies* the existence of it, if you can believe it. "I do not buy the concept, popular in the '60s, which said, 'We have suppressed the black man for 300 years and the white man is now far ahead in the race for everything our society offers. In order to even the score, we must now give the black man a head start, or even hold the white man back, to even the race.' I don't buy that," Biden said to a weekly newspaper in Delaware in 1975. "I don't feel responsible for the sins of my father and grandfather. I feel responsible for what the situation is today, for the sins of my own generation. And I'll be damned if I feel responsible to pay for what happened 300 years ago."

This confusing and deceptive dynamic with the black community—portraying himself as a hero of the people while simultaneously showing his blatant disregard and disrespect for the historically embedded systemic racism of our country and how it has disproportionately affected African Americans—started his long history of telling the black constituency he can be trusted, while simultaneously authoring and implementing policies that would hurt them.

In fact, dating back to the 1970s, Biden started his tenure in Congress cozying up to the institutional power that was in the Senate at the time, including Senator James O. Eastland of Mississippi, a segregationist, who helped Biden gain seats at the table on the committees and subcommittees overseeing criminal justice and prison reform, and the aforementioned Thurmond. These two segregationist senators controlled many of the levers of power a newly sworn-in Biden would need to become an effective legislator and seem to have influenced his policy-making decisions over the decades as well.

Nowadays, and for decades past, Biden's favorite tagline has been to peddle how in touch he is with black communities, but what has actually been the case is that Biden has built up some level of trust and comfort with his black constituency only to simultaneously turn around and publicly contradict it once he was in a position of power. Over the years, his connections to black leaders and his service as Barack

Obama's vice president have endeared him to older conservative African Americans who may feel comfortable with him after what he touts as years of service in their name. He's a familiar name to the black community by now, and at the start of the 2020 race for the Democratic nomination, this gave him an impressive lead in the polls among this crucial constituency to the Democratic Party. Polls showed he consistently had over 40 percent of the African American vote nationally, and surveys from South Carolina, the first southern state to vote and one with a high percentage of black voters, showed Biden scoring even higher than that.

Biden's argument for why he should be the 2020 Democratic nominee for president was that he's the steady, experienced, and safe choice to take on Donald Trump and has the deepest connections to black communities. The warm feelings many voters, particularly black voters, have for Biden is because of his proximity to Barack Obama. But in the 2020 primary race, his own record was considered separately from the president he served, and that reality is a bit more complicated because, as Biden proudly flaunts his connections with black communities, he and his campaign have also displayed no honest accounting or rectifying of the damage he's already done *to* these nonwhite populations. So far, he still does not seem open to that level of self-examination and reflection. He has his own complicity in criminalizing black and brown people. He has managed to earn the black community's trust over time despite having written the infamous 1994 crime bill, the Violent Crime Control and Law Enforcement Act, signed into law by President Bill Clinton, which is credited with creating America's epidemic of mass incarceration. During the Democratic primary, Biden tried to downplay his association with this bill's effects on communities, but the history of it and his associations with the aforesaid segregationists who were in power at the time has put him at odds with a growing base of the Democratic electorate who have no patience for any rationalization of these harmful policies.

The consequences of the 1994 crime bill have been devastating for communities of color. This draconian bill, which put into place stiff penalties for drug offenses, exploded the American prison population, which grew exponentially over the next twenty-five years. These arrests targeted drugs that were common in black and brown communities, such as crack cocaine, while allowing for lighter penalties—or no penalties at all—for drug arrests more common in white communities, including prescription drug abuse, which ballooned into the opioid crisis, while black and brown people are still being jailed for marijuana. There are nearly 1.65 million people incarcerated on the state and federal level in the United States, and the vast majority of those behind bars are black and Latino. To put this in perspective, there are more black men incarcerated in America right now than were enslaved during America's four hundred years of chattel slavery. Mass incarceration destroys entire communities. When one person is removed from the home, the damaging repercussions can be felt generations later. Joe Biden is the unapologetic author of this bill, showing just how Republican some of his policies really are.

Young voters—those who didn't live through the economic prosperity of the 1990s as adults and, thus, don't hold this up as an icon of a favorable and progressive presidential era— *do* see Bill Clinton's 1994 Violent Crime Control and Law Enforcement Act as the legislation that created the current

THE BLUE WAVE IS NOT UNCLE JOE

crisis of mass incarceration that scholar Michelle Alexander described in her book *The New Jim Crow: Mass Incarceration in the Age of Colorblindness*. The crime bill increased federal sentences, expanded America's war on drugs (first initiated by Richard Nixon in response to drug abuse being "public enemy number one" for Americans), and even funded the building of even more prisons. Biden must own the legacy of his damaging legislation, which has exacerbated racial inequality in America and gutted entire families and neighborhoods, a fact he fails to acknowledge, even as he holds out his hand and asks for the black and brown vote from people whose families were—and are still being—negatively and disproportionately impacted by his policies.

Around the same time President Clinton signed the 1994 crime bill into law, Biden was quoted as saying from the floor: "The truth is every major crime bill since 1976 that's come out of this Congress, every minor crime bill, has had the name of the Democratic senator from the State of Delaware: Joe Biden." Such statements are being remembered today by younger constituents as they see the impact of his bills on their communities. They didn't need to live through these impactful events as adults to feel their vibrations in their communities now. Biden's argument for why he should be the 2020 Democratic nominee for president was also an argument for normalization. It was a refusal to admit the past wasn't great for people of color and that simply clinging to the status quo is unacceptable for communities of color, especially after their political power has grown. His entire thesis ignored the fact that the stereotypes about black and brown people have always been there and that he has done nothing to combat them with his own policies. In fact, he ignored his own complicity in criminalizing black and brown people in the first place. That's the framework for our politics.

For those voters of color who know and understand Biden's history, his presence in American politics represents an internal struggle of which version of Joe they'll get if they cast their ballot for him and he wins the presidential election. Will they get the tough-on-crime Joe or Uncle Joe who stood by the first black president's side for eight years and who launched the radical initiative "It's On Us" with the White House Council on Women and Girls? This policy was the first of its kind, tackling the epidemic of campus sexual assault. It is great for the women who get to college, but what about other young women who don't? Would Biden be a president who'd look out for their needs too? Would he be a president who could take on their challenges? That's what must be asked of Biden.

It's ultimately a question of trust. Trust in politics is earned through results, whether those results are negative or positive. Biden is either in denial of the damage he's done to these communities or completely unaware of it. I'm not sure which is worse, but I do know that it's not something that should be ignored. These are the sorts of things that people of color need to consider deeply when looking at a candidate—not just what they say on camera but what their policies say about them.

Experienced politicians like Biden who defend the good parts of their records but don't acknowledge the damage they've done come across as disingenuous to those communities that are directly impacted. In a post–Black Lives Matter world, where racial justice and even reparations for the ancestors of enslaved black people are a normal part of a presidential debate conversation, race and justice for those who have for generations been treated as less than white Americans, incarcerated, and even killed when unarmed are not issues that the people can afford to pass over.

Senator Kamala Harris faced immense scrutiny for her record as a prosecutor, but the difference between Harris and Biden is that Harris was operating under the laws that Biden wrote. She was following his law. They both can and should be held accountable for the consequences, but there is a hierarchy and chain of command between legislation and prosecution. For both legislators and prosecutors, an apology should be step one. A comprehensive plan to roll back the impacts of mass incarceration through record expungements, financial investments into communities impacted, and an open line of communication in case the solutions proposed and implemented aren't effective should follow immediately after.

The first Democratic primary debate for the 2020 nomination was a sign of problems down the road for Biden: if not immediately evident in his polling with younger black voters, it was a sign that initially, enthusiasm for his candidacy was complicated. Though he started out as the assumed frontrunner of the race, that strength seemed to weaken as the primary voting began and as Bernie Sanders clocked in win after win in the caucuses. Biden's more moderate approach to public policy required compromise. It's easy to say "progress is incremental" when your community is not the one suffering under slow changes. This was a vulnerability of his platform and his campaign that demonstrated the weakness in the older establishment Democrats' ability to engage younger generations.

Joe Biden comes from a different era, one which doesn't naturally fit in this generation of forward progressivism and which often rejects mainstream liberalism. Biden represents another generation of political power, one that hinged on moderation and incremental change rather than big-idea policy to push the nation forward. Biden's politics represent the past. With an existential threat like Donald Trump in the Oval Office, Biden's desire to maintain the status quo comes up short for what the moment requires.

Biden's primary claim about why he's the man for the job is that he's the one who can rebuild the Obama coalition and take advantage of those same voting blocs because he was Obama's righthand man. He can bring us back to the way things were pre-2016—the way things were under Obama. The message is that Americans can trust good old Uncle Joe because he can bring us back to the status quo. But the reality is that the status quo back then was still subpar for the margins of American society. Trayvon Martin was killed by George Zimmerman when Obama was president. Eric Garner was strangled by the NYPD on camera when Obama was president. Sandra Bland died under questionable circumstances in a Texas jail cell when Obama was president. None of them saw justice. The system was broken then, and it's broken now. So, forget going back. Ole Uncle Joe needs to be talking about how to push us forward, not how to keep people of color stagnant.

The Great Recession hit communities of color particularly hard, and upon reflection, President Obama's economic policies brought America back from the brink, but that doesn't mean that black and brown families—not to mention the Millennial generation—weren't hit like a ton of bricks by the financial meltdown and, particularly, the mortgage crisis that precipitated the crash. Although Obama tried to get the economy off life support through the Recovery Act, Republican obstruction prevented a lot of additional steps his administration could have taken to directly help these same communities. Biden's strength is his experience, but with experience comes this type of baggage that voters should hold him accountable for.

And the days of Democratic leaders *not* showing up for us go back decades, as Senator Kamala Harris pointed out. She was the first person to reveal Biden's weakness as a candidate after online buzz ignited around old newspaper clippings of Joe Biden talking about busing with segregationists who were still in the US Congress. Those quotes revealed that he found busing, the act of the government forcing students to racially integrate in public schools, to be intrusive and bad for his own children.

"It was actually harmful to hear you talk about the reputations of two United States senators who built their [careers] on the segregation of race in this country," Harris told Biden. "It was not only that, but you also worked with them to oppose busing. There was a little girl in California who was part of the second class to integrate her public schools. She was bused to school every day. That little girl was me."

White moderates, including Biden, criticized government-mandated busing as inconvenient and unfair to white parents who didn't want their children to attend school with little black children like Kamala Harris. Harris is a living busing success story. It wasn't about Biden having the wrong opinion; it was about "moderates" like Biden accounting for some of the negative policy outcomes they've contributed to.

Biden struggled to respond in any coherent way whatsoever. Katie Glueck, reporter for the *New York Times*, characterized his response, in a September 15, 2019, article, as "a rambling, discordant answer to a question about the legacy of slavery, a moment that highlighted his unsteady instincts, and mixed record, on matters of race." He even seemed to defend his outdated position of opposing busing back in the day. His failure to acknowledge what he had done while standing on the stage with a black woman who was directly impacted by the policies was a terrible move. Senator Harris brought up an honest conversation that we, as a party, can't be afraid to tackle head on.

In fact, Biden's stumbles reminded me of one of the early mistakes we made on the Hillary campaign on a day I will forever refer to as Superpredator Day—the day that Black Lives Matter protesters confronted Hillary Clinton at a fundraiser in South Carolina and demanded an apology for her referring to gang members as "superpredators" in a 1996 speech she made supporting the 1994 crime bill. The same crime bill authored by Biden. The superpredator confrontation was captured on video and went viral online. Hillary's 1996 comment is now seen as a racist description of young black men, and while academia was the first place to use the term, it came back around to haunt us from my first day on the campaign to my last.

One day after Hillary lost the New Hampshire primary to Bernie Sanders, going into the South Carolina primary, I got a message from one of my friends, Matt Ortega, who was already working on the campaign. He said that his boss wanted to talk to me, and they wanted to offer me a job. I'd worked for Obama in 2008 but hadn't planned on working on the campaign side in the 2016 cycle. The Hillary Clinton campaign offered me a job on the first call. I was hired because I have a pulse on #BlackTwitter, and I went into the campaign with a mission.

An apology for saying "superpredators" was basically number one on my list of things to get Hillary to do when I arrived. The South Carolina primary was looming, and it would be the first primary where the black community would have a loud voice and large numbers. I knew that this quote from 1996 could dog the campaign with important groups of voters. And, honestly, it just wasn't great that she had said this, despite the full context of the situation. Since I am very plugged in to both black media and social justice activism through my media work, I was in a good position to assess the campaign's need to quickly address some of these issues, but I had to run those concerns up through the chain of command. In no way was I the only person on the campaign with this ability, but I was absolutely someone who could identify problems quickly, an invaluable resource to most campaigns, especially on the presidential level.

When I first saw the video of Hillary being confronted in South Carolina, I had just started on the campaign. And although I was new, I was the person most likely to understand how fast the confrontation would become a problem and that it wouldn't go away just because we didn't talk about it. The campaign manager insisted the controversy would blow over, but my gut told me it was going to be a nonstop cable news story for the next twenty-four hours, at the very least. As our campaign call wrapped up, I had this gnawing in my stomach that told me I should say something. I chose not to, buckling under the scrutiny of my newness. The next day, the story blew up all over cable news, solidifying the narrative that Hillary had called all black men superpredators and that she wasn't sorry about it either. What a mess. That was the last time I ever hesitated before speaking up for the rest of the campaign, and it shows just how damaging these moments can be to candidates—moments like this of which Biden has had plenty.

Watching the campaign struggle to respond to the blowup was a big lesson for me because I realized how my generation sees the crime bill as an egregious dark spot on American legislation—the cause of mass incarceration and the visible thief of the humanity of every person who's ever been addicted to drugs or sucked into gang warfare. The lesson here is that presidential candidates can't pretend like the weaknesses in their records or their past statements won't come back around to bite them. Biden is, in many ways, in the same place Hillary was in this superpredator moment. She did eventually apologize, and she continued to talk about how she was going to fix the damaging consequences of the crime bill, but Biden has yet to grasp that he has a closing window of time to properly account for his mistakes and close the divide he has with this generation and racial demographic of voters.

His debate gaffe demonstrated that he still has his own blind spots on how race issues of the past play in today's climate, an issue that nonwhite candidates of the future are less likely to have. The consequences of his past legislative policies require an evolution on Biden's part as he steps into being our Democratic nominee against Trump. To create a winning coalition, Biden must learn the lessons from 2016 and approach race issues and the aftermath of his policies head on. He must avoid becoming Hillary 2.0 and avoid augmenting the already present generational divide. The fact of the matter is that this generation understands how damaging the crime bill and the affront to busing and other policies of Biden's have been for communities of color. Biden likely has to own these outcomes even more than Hillary did in her campaign because he *authored* the legislation that did so much damage. And that damage isn't only being felt in the past tense; there are people in prison right now who are there because of Joe Biden's crime bill, and there are families that will never be the same as a result of his policies.

The progressive movement's leadership and our presidential candidates must reflect not only the diversity of the voters who will win them the elections but the diversity of our country as well. Biden can't ignore the damage he has caused. Attracting black and brown Millennial and Gen Z voters isn't going to be easy, but Biden has to decide how he will speak to this very imperative demographic, rather than simply ignoring that they exist and that his policy decisions have affected them. And speaking to them with the moderation of an establishment Democrat will make his road all the more of an uphill battle, particularly with the verbiage he has used throughout the race for the nomination, touting himself as a hero of black people, positioned to commiserate with their struggles, as if he could be the savior of these communities if they would only give him the vote.

Black communities don't need a white savior, even if well meaning. These communities need money and resources. Knowing black people and *seeing* us aren't the same thing. When you really see black people, you see the discrimination and disrespect we face daily that's built on decades of systemic bigotry and that always places us a few laps behind people who aren't any more or less deserving of those resources than we are. Too often folks in power think that the solutions come from them waxing poetic about the sad ills of communities of color couched in language like "delivering" for those communities. Rarely do you hear that same verbiage used for other demographics of people, and the distinction does matter. These communities are self-sufficient when provided with enough investment and resources. The race divide is the gap between the understanding these older white Democrats have for the people who live in those communities and what solutions will actually help them self-determine their lives in a real and substantive way.

The message that the establishment took away from the 2018 midterm election's blue wave is that "moderate" is the only way to win suburban voters over. But that's the wrong message for a Democratic takeaway. When Democratic candidates won in historically red and purple districts with high populations of Republican voters, they *didn't* win by being just like Republicans and by supporting Republican-style policies as Biden has. They didn't win by trying to stay as close to the middle as they could. They won by responding directly to the needs of their constituents. Issues like health care are the most pressing, but the cost of housing and a complete lack of affordable childcare or paid family leave are issues that Democrats are in the perfect position to speak on. Yet, Biden doesn't demonstrate, in his rhetoric or through his policies, that he sees a need for any big structural changes that may be necessary to get our government working for *every* American of *every* background. He doesn't speak directly to policies such as reproductive health care access and the Hyde Amendment, which bans usage of Medicaid for abortion services. This law blocks women from abortions if they are too poor to pay for one.

Reproductive access impacts lower-income communities more than middle-class, upper-middle-class, and rich communities. *Access* is the most important word when it comes to reproductive health care. Without access, the *right* to an abortion, for example, isn't real. And without affordable access, a *right* might as well not be a right at all—if only people with means can benefit from it. Early in his run for president, Biden's initial support of the Hyde Amendment (he has since switched his position) came under scrutiny because it clearly showed that the issues that matter to underprivileged women didn't matter to him.

The current progressive movement—and certainly the Millennials and Zs—understand that the Hyde Amendment is discriminatory in its impact. Women who can't afford to pay for an abortion do not have access to one, even though it is their legal right to obtain one. This is especially an issue for women of color, who are more likely to be insured by Medicaid, leaving them with hundreds of dollars in out-of-pocket costs.

Biden's old-school moderation on policies makes him an asymmetrical leader in a time demanding more. The blue wave of 2018 didn't happen because the candidates clung to centrist ideology to gain moderate or typically Republican voters. Instead, they made a clear argument for themselves based on identity politics. For example, Representative Katie Porter of California's candidacy is just one of many that demonstrates how pandering to the middle as Joe Biden does isn't the way to win today's elections. In her campaign, Porter openly talked about being a survivor of domestic violence, challenging special interest groups, and holding the powerful accountable for their policies. Her own experience informed the policies she proposed, like a provision in the Violence

Against Women Act that deals with economic abuse she her-self experienced firsthand.

When Porter is ensuring that economic harassment is in-cluded in a bill providing resources for victims of domestic violence, it's because her lived experiences better inform her policy making. That is what democracy is all about. The gov-ernment works *for* us. How is Joe Biden's policy working for the people? His 1994 crime bill has disproportionately landed men of color in prison for at least a generation and his early support of the Hyde Amendment disproportionately affected poor women, even if he's more recently changed his tune.

We need a bolder vision than looking back because there is no time in the past where women and people of color col-lectively have had more power than we do right now. So why would we want to "go back" to the way things were? Why would we want to regress our lives, our policies, and our im-pact on world politics when we fought so hard to progress them? Biden's entire thesis of being the candidate who can take us back is an ideology that is MAGA-like, dangerously close to the same sounding boards that gave us Trump. Young voters of color don't want to go back to anything; we want to go forward with a government that looks like us. Be-sides, there was no pre-Trump period of all rainbows and flowers. We want to progress toward a more equitable future. We want a future that radically reimagines American society, a future that requires a leader to speak truth to power about the present and past with an actual understanding of the cost of a gallon of milk in our neighborhoods—and whether or not that's even affordable.

Though it's not surprising that many black voters over the age of forty immediately defaulted to the vice president they know—a man associated with a black president they love—early in the primary process, instead of hitching their support to a candidate who is lesser known, we must stop this way of thinking. We must look deeper into a candidate's politics. A 2020 win by association with the first black president isn't a win at all.

Democrats should use the electoral process to challenge and deeply evaluate everyone. Surviving a thorough vetting makes any candidate stronger for the general election, should he or she make it that far. Each time Biden is tested, he can prove to those voters of color that he has learned from past missteps by having formulated new plans to clean up his mess and show a willingness to evolve. And if elected, he should agree to be held fully accountable.

Biden can't defend the crime bill, and Bloomberg couldn't defend stop and frisk. Mayor Pete couldn't defend his handling of the police brutality cases against his black constituents. And the candidates we elect now and forevermore should not try. They have to pivot to what they are going to do to *make up for* these mistakes and be serious about making amends. And they have to do that every day, in every interview, and behave as if the voters who have been bamboozled in the past can now trust them to do no harm in the future. And that's step one of many.

Hillary Clinton did this as a centerpiece to her campaign. Not only did Hillary begin her campaign with a speech about criminal justice reform, but once when asked about the harm to communities of color, Hillary also took the moment to apologize again in an interview with NY1's Errol Louis. When asked, "Do you regret your advocacy for the crime bill?" Hillary said, "I'm sorry for the consequences that were unintended and that have had a very unfortunate impact on people's lives. I've seen the results of what has happened in families and in communities. That's why I chose to make my very first speech a year ago on this issue, Errol [Louis], because I want to focus the attention of our country, and to make the changes we need to make. I also want people, especially, I want white people, I want white people to recognize that there is systemic racism. It's also in employment. It's in housing, but it is in the criminal justice system as well." Unfortunately, this kind of apology from politicians just doesn't happen very often.

As noted earlier, Maya Harris was a senior policy adviser for Hillary Clinton's campaign. Her background in criminal justice and her work as the president of the ACLU of Northern California made her our point person for all things criminal justice reform, among so many other critical issues. Coming from that background—and even, interestingly, as one of the people who helped edit *The New Jim Crow*—Harris, no doubt, advised Clinton to respond to these mistakes she'd made from a position of reflection instead of attempting to constantly defend the indefensible.

The generational divide between what younger black voters knew about Clinton's record and what voters over the age of forty knew could not have been more different. Older voters then, similar to Biden's support base now, didn't demand an apology and complete accounting for the disparate impact that the crime bill had had on communities of color—that it's had on their own children and cousins and friends. As is the case in many bad relationships, what those voters remembered most were the good ole days of Bill Clinton's administration. As my own mom said to me back in 2016, "We support

Hillary because when her husband was president, black people had jobs and the economy was great." Unfortunately, this sentiment was not shared by younger voters of color, a constituency that Clinton's 2016 presidential campaign was unable to inspire enough to vote for the Democrats.

This was an issue for Joe Biden's 2020 primary campaign as well. Older voters of color remember when he *was* there for them more than when he *wasn't*. The times he wasn't is where his campaign should have started as opposed to leaning into the warm nostalgic feelings we, as black Americans, have for the Obama years. Biden is now running on his own record, and that record, coupled with his inability to speak to black and brown communities on racial issues when prompted, will be his political downfall if he doesn't rectify it, and soon. Because, let me make something clear: despite what Biden believes, white Americans *have* had over a three-hundred-year head start in this country, so it's time for everyone else to catch up. And the starting line is the ballot box.

CHAPTER 8

The Billionaire
Boys' Club

A MERICANS ARE STRUGGLING EVERYWHERE.
Wages have been stagnant for decades. Everyone is working hard trying to get ahead, to make a comfortable life for themselves and for their families outside the land of the one percentile. Yet, Americans from all walks of life need a little help to make the hard work they are doing pay off to the utmost extent. Wealth disparity in America has hit an all-time high. In late 2019, the US Census Bureau reported that income inequality in the United States, as measured by the Gini index, reached the highest level it's seen in more than fifty years. We now live in a world where, for the first time in US history, America's wealthiest four hundred families pay a lower effective tax rate than any other income group, including the working class. And since the financial, political, and social systems currently in place are so often rigged to favor those who are already in power—from tax loopholes for the wealthy to education and wealth gaps created by the well-off's abundance of resources compared to the masses—we need a reimagining of how resources are allocated to communities so that everyday Americans are able to self-determine and set up the next generation to be just a little bit more secure than this one.

The gap between the rich and the working poor in America has never been wider, yet the Democratic Party has moved away from its core post–civil rights values of being the party for working people and families. This is the moment to pivot back to our foundational principles. Since the financial crash in 2008, which led to the Great Recession, the Occupy Wall Street movement has put the issue of income inequality into the mainstream consciousness. In 2011, thousands of protesters camped out in Zuccotti Park in lower Manhattan for months, demanding that the powers-that-be listen to the concerns of the bottom 99 percent of income earners who had been gutted by Wall Street's recklessness and deregulation. Occupy Wall Street created a radical shift in the awareness and coverage of income equality as an issue that needs to be solved with some urgency. While the protest movement shifted the public conversation, it didn't build a political movement to shape any future legislation. And while income inequality itself is colorblind, the effect of historically classist and racist structures—such as gerrymandering and redlining—have left generations a lap behind their fellow Americans. If there was an intentional legislative way to get us into this mess, such as the aforementioned practices, then that means there must be intentional legislative action to right the ship.

In many ways, our very own president represents the excesses that the occupy movement railed against—the very excesses and power-hungry greed that brought this nation to its knees only a decade ago, causing the collapse of the housing market. He represents the one percentile, which has separated itself so effectively from the rest of the country that this single percentile now owns more collective wealth than the bottom 90 percent of America. The entire brand of Donald Trump—going back to the 1980s—is one of decadence and literal gold lamé. The gilded lifestyle of the Trumps was one that blue-collar people aspired to, especially as they watched him broadcast his superficially fabulous life worldwide on his reality television show *The Apprentice*. When you see Trump, you see excess. Too much gold. Too much exuberance. Too little taste. In some ways, this masterstroke of marketing blinded voters to the reality that Trump, himself, is a failed businessman buoyed by his father's passed-down millions, which he used as start-up money for his series of failed businesses. He is neither self-made nor a self-starter. He is only a failed product of generational wealth that most Americans don't have access to.

The contradiction is obvious: Trump's perceived persona of success collides with his true persona and the reality of his repeated bankruptcies. Such a history doesn't exactly scream out that he's an "expert business mogul." Trump University, his namesake educational institution, was sued for fraud. His charity, the Donald J. Trump Foundation, was fined for his misuse of the charity foundation; he has admitted to using the funds to bolster his own campaign financing and settle personal debts. (I repeat, this is a man who is on record as having *misused* charitable contributions in a fraudulent way.) He has a long history of not paying people who complete work for him, including contractors and vendors—*actual* working-class people—whom he left high and dry during the years of the Great Recession when he bought up property like it was a Monopoly board game in cities like Atlanta, Georgia. As soon as the market turned and the real estate bubble popped, leaving him with entire blocks of property midway through construction, he then deserted these projects, refusing to pay his contractors and their laborers for their hard work. As a result, this man has been sued more times than Eminem. The Trump Organization has been frequently sued for back pay, as he's also in the habit of only paying his contractors for half the agreed-upon fees after the job is completed. It's public record that he has been sued for this.

But these facts don't seem to coexist with the myth that Trump has created about himself, which allowed him to waltz into the White House in the first place. It's important to understand that Trump's appeal to working-class people is based on a lie that he's one of them, that he understands their pain, and that he cares for them. His "populist" and often class-based message was and is completely false. He doesn't care for the people, and he's on record for his shady dealings, which have *hurt* the same people who turned around and voted for him. But he's constructed a brilliant shiny mirror to hide behind. Trump pits whites against everyone else to avoid drawing attention to his own past, which is completely antithetical to his working-man message. The core of "American anxiety," the media-driven notion that helped propel him to office, isn't economics; it's a race-based, self-interested ideology that contends whites don't already have a full claim to every resource America has to offer unopposed. And the new leader and face of this message is none other than Trump himself.

The media loves to say that Donald Trump's 2016 campaign magically turned out a hidden white working-class vote, but the misconception about Trump's base of support is that they are working class. The most common trait among Trump voters isn't their class status; it's the color of their skin. The threat to their social and political dominance—at least, as they perceived it during the first black presidency and, subsequently, at the possibility of the first female presidency—is somewhat existential. Almost like America's primal scream. Trump appealed to white economic anxiety and fears by giving those voters someone to blame. He turned their heads away from the social and legislative issues at hand and, instead, scapegoated immigrants and communities of color as the cause of white America's pain. Laid off? Undocumented immigrants are to blame because they are perceived as the ones who are "stealing jobs." Afraid of terrorists? Muslims are to blame because it is these Islamic countries that have set their sights indiscriminately on the US for attack. Trump referred to immigrants from the continent of Africa as people who are coming from shithole countries. He added that America would really benefit from more immigrants coming from Norway, which is a not-so-subtle message that immigrants from white countries are somehow more worthy or superior than immigrants from countries full of black people.

This divide along race lines is the way Donald Trump exploits that anxiety, creating a feeling of resentment toward groups who are deemed "other." He gets white voters to channel their anxiety into resentment toward communities of color and toward campaigns that speak to their racist fears. The Trump voters fed into the narrative that people of color were the problem. But the 2020 election provides an opportunity to be honest about the lie Trump perpetuated—the idea that he represents the working man, or even that the working man voted for him as some sort of waking silent majority that was so eager to hear someone speaking to their economic issues. That's revisionist history.

That Trump's core supporters happen not to all be rich isn't the point. He's speaking to them bluntly and pointing away from himself and toward other convenient enemies: people of color, immigrants, and the left-wing media, which doesn't spew his rhetoric. What everyone misses when discussing Trump is that racism is the main feature, not a sideshow or quirk. He lives in gilded towers and mocks those he deems weak and vulnerable. He isn't a champion for the working-class voter, and he's never once even shown he cares about them in actual practice in his personal life before the presidency either.

Real-life experiences matter. If you have the lived experience of a working-class person, you understand the real-life consequences of public policy, and you know how much of an impact additional resources can have on historically marginalized people so that they at least have an equal shot at the American pie. But in Trump's limited and highly privileged worldview, the regular people don't register at all when he's doing the day-to-day work of the presidency. And who said anything about giving *everyone* an equal shot, anyway?

Racial and social justice issues are intimately intertwined in all aspects of Americans' ability to get ahead and take care of their families. So, the messaging that Democrats think will attract white working-class voters actually turns off working-class voters who are *not* white. This practice of robbing Peter to pay Paul sends a bad signal to voters of color that Democrats don't see. To cultivate a winning message, the economic messaging must include the recognition that systemic oppression impacts outcomes for different demographics of people. The Trump voters accepted the narrative that people of color were the problem, but Democrats cannot also fall into this trap. The bedrock of the Democratic Party is made up of people of color, and those voters are repelled by messages that speak to Trump's voters who are *anti* people of color. The demographic math clearly shows more Democratic opportunities for victory by leaning into a message of justice and equity for all, not by trying to woo Trump voters to our side through messaging geared toward antiminority sentiments or tolerance.

By trying to deny that the people who voted for and currently support Donald Trump weren't, at the very least, tolerant of his racist messaging is a stretch of the imagination and a slap in the face to all of the millions of Americans who were offended by it. How does it really sound, from the perspective of a nonwhite person, if a white Democrat says, "Trump voters weren't racist; they just had a little bout of economic anxiety. That's all," while at the same time, Trump is announcing a Muslim ban, calling white supremacists "fine people," and caging brown toddlers on the southern border who are barely old enough to talk, let alone break laws?

Going forward, the party must reframe the conversation and give black and brown voters at all socioeconomic levels the same care and attention that they give white voters. Break down their issue areas and concerns. What do they need and want, and how can the party put forward plans to address those concerns? Do they have a lack of access to affordable health care and housing? If so, then what's our plan to fix it?

That's why new congresspeople like Alexandria Ocasio-Cortez are so refreshing. AOC's A Just Society legislation is important because it hearkens back to periods in history where the focus in the civil rights community was on antipoverty proposals that would unite people of all races around class issues. AOC understands that class is not an isolated identity that has no relationship to other parts of a person's identity. Like her first proposal, the Green New Deal, this new antipoverty proposal is intended to further our society as well. Her bills would open social benefits to all people, even undocumented immigrants.

In A Just Society, AOC calls for a change to the way the federal government measures who is poor and who is living in poverty. In a tweet announcing the package, she wrote, "Did you know our Fed[eral] poverty line is based on 1955 spending, & the way we calculate it hasn't changed since 1964? It assumes 1 earner & a mother home full-time. It doesn't include the cost of childcare, geographic cost of living, or health care. Some predict it should be *$38k/yr.*" That measurement of the national federal poverty line, she thinks, should be higher for a lot of American families. The current formula puts the poverty line at an annual salary of $12,500, which leaves out millions of American families who are really struggling with stagnant wages and the rising costs of living. She also considers geographic location in how we measure the poverty line and the distribution of federal dollars to various parts of the country. It should depend on where you live because that absolutely matters. If you live in a rural community, your rent isn't going to match someone living in Brooklyn. The cost of living in New York City or San Francisco is totally different than the cost of living in, say, Tulsa, Oklahoma, and yet there's no recognition of this in our federal code.

If the calculation is changed, more Americans would be able to benefit from the security of government resources like housing, food assistance, welfare, and Medicaid. She doesn't exclude Americans with criminal records from seeking out this kind of assistance under this new formula, and she also doesn't exclude undocumented immigrants. In AOC's worldview, every single human being shouldn't be too poor to live. AOC has lived some of the very same experiences she's now fighting against with her legislation and knows what it means to live paycheck to paycheck, battle against the foreclosure of her parents' house, and feel overwhelmed by crippling student loan debt. She understands working people, and her legislative package demonstrates that she's committed to being one of our loudest voices and champions in Congress by centering on an accurate description of how we really live.

The working-class people of America do need a voice in the Democratic Party and legislation. If candidates come up with the messaging and a policy framework to address the specific needs of working-class voters of color—those same communities that represent an emerging majority of American voters—these communities will turn out to support them, too. That's how identity-based politics stands up to classism.

The focus on class without considering the other identities that contribute to the disparity in American economic outcomes is one shortcoming of the current Democratic establishment. But that's only half the battle, and it will only happen if our candidates themselves feel the value in it. They can't just be less racist than Trump, or less overtly racist, if we are being really honest. The entire framework for building lasting political power in the future is about centering the most marginalized or, as Angela Davis says, to be "antiracist," and it's a known fact in today's America that race and class *do* intersect in significant ways.

People aren't poor in a vacuum. And they aren't poor by accident either. They aren't simply lazy, and most of the working-class people in the country are people who work. They are simply in jobs that don't pay enough in a country that costs too much. Everyone wants their children to have a better life than the one they did, but when student loan debt is the only path to higher education, these families are two or three generations away from economic stability. And some also have to deal with the legacy of gender and race caste systems. Those systems don't allow for people to get ahead. The idea that people with a lot of money have those resources because they work harder than those punching time cards for minimum wage is one of the biggest lies America tells itself. The amount of money you make isn't a virtue or evidence of moral character. And even if you are lucky enough to make enough money to buy a home or some other feature of the promised American dream, all freedoms aren't guaranteed to all people.

Black and brown Americans know that having money isn't any kind of guarantee of physical safety, fairness, or even economic mobility. Survival shouldn't be this hard. Democrats need to lean into the message that we are the party that is there to make life a little easier. In his book *The Audacity of Hope*, Barack Obama described the difference between Republicans and Democrats. He said that Republicans tend to go into government to seek power and to set themselves up for lobbying positions once they are out of office. Basically, they are in it for the power and the money. Democrats, on the other hand, tend to go into higher office to help people. The next wave of Democrats post-Trump should focus on that core value and lean into the fact that the more people they seek to help through policies and protection, the more support they will likely enjoy going forward. It also happens to be the right thing to do.

Many black and brown voters know what it's like to be working class. It goes back to the time when domestic workers in the South organized the bus boycotts that would later ignite the civil rights movement. Black women in particular—those who spent their days as domestic workers and service employees—activated their entire communities in protest. They printed and handed out flyers so that everyone in their communities would get the directive. These women have always been working class, but you never see journalists go to talk to them in a diner. And that's the problem.

Women of color especially make up a large percentage of teachers, domestic workers, and minimum-wage workers in the United States. These women of color are the ones who most desperately need policy changes to improve their lives because, even if they match dollar for dollar with a white person's working-class salary, they still have to combat the skin-color prejudice that's been written into our society and our legislation. The racist narratives that allow Republican politicians to constantly cut funding to programs that would help these working women on a day-to-day basis are the same ones that scare Democrats away from offering alternatives that explicitly mention race for fear of alienating too many white voters. Not to mention, white people statistically receive more government aid and welfare than any other demographic in the nation, though you wouldn't know it from the racist propaganda that's been circulated for decades.

These voters have been invisible to the traditional power structures. They are working-class people, too, and their votes and their voices matter. Black women have been working class for generations, and they require targeted policies that address their deepest concerns. The social justice issues at hand in America today are also economic issues that impact these demographics. Abortion and access to reproductive health care are economic issues for American women and families. The choice of when, how, and under what circumstances to have children is a decision about money. The majority of women who seek abortions in America already have children and cite economic realities as the reason for seeking the medical procedure. Access to contraception care is also an economic decision for women and families. A woman who isn't able to self-determine her own life isn't fully free. And with that freedom to choose is the ability to plan financially, something every adult in America should be able to understand.

When *Roe v. Wade* wasn't the law of the land and abortion was illegal, affluent white women were still able to access abortions with their private doctors. Poor women did not have that privilege simply because they didn't have enough money. They died in back alleys after taking drastic measures to secure abortions or even died in childbirth. American women now are standing in the gap between the future and the past that took so many women's lives. This is an issue that connects the generations and the races because we do not want to go back to a time when the lives of women were put at risk and we didn't have control over our own bodies and destinies. If *Roe* is overturned by the US Supreme Court, millions of American women—and certainly the most marginalized of them—will be set back decades, as if this monumental law had never been enacted in the first place. A woman's ability to self-determine is severely limited when her freedom over her own reproduction is snatched away. This fight is, essentially, about whether or not women have the same freedom over their own destinies as men do and whether poor women have the same freedom over their own destinies as more privileged women do—and that's an issue that takes a collective coalition to fight and win, an issue that urgently calls for intersectionality and identity politics.

Affordable childcare is something that would transform entire communities. Representative Ilhan Omar, newly elected off the 2018 blue wave, recognized this and did something about it, empowering the federal-government-employed families who were substantially harmed by the partisan bickering and the consequential 2018 government shutdown. Many of those federal contractors, who were forced to go to work for no money during the political fight, would have been left holding the bag were it not for Omar's legislation to compensate them for their labor.

Omar's first bill in Congress was written to provide childcare and compensation to the families directly impacted by the shutdown. If childcare costs more than your paycheck, then what's the point in going to work at all? By providing them with affordable childcare, they at least have the security of knowing that they aren't losing money every time they go to work. The lack of access to affordable childcare is one of the most fundamental class issues of today, and, according to Omar, quality and affordable childcare should be a right, not a privilege.

Moderation and Money Don't Mix

Here's a fun fact: rich people fund elections. They put money behind candidates, and they sit at fancy dinners with white tablecloths chatting and golf clapping through bland baked chicken breasts and unlimited wine. Big money rules the day in Washington because the more money a candidate has, the better chance he or she has of winning an election. We may see politicians shaking hands on the campaign trail, but their dirty secret is that political campaigning is incredibly choreographed and the big money donors—the ones who pour millions and millions into fueling a candidate's campaign— are the ones who get the most face time with the candidates. If candidates are always spending time with rich people and chatting with them about *their* most pressing concerns, then whose perspective of the world and what it needs do you think these candidates will internalize?

We need an honest accounting of the malicious influence of money in our politics. The influence of money in politics both stems from and perpetuates class issues in America. Even in the 2020 race for the Democratic nomination, we have seen billionaires self-financing their own runs for president, like Democratic candidates Tom Steyer and Michael Bloomberg, creating a financial imbalance and putting the other candidates at a disadvantage, because they could not keep their campaigns running for as long as these rich and powerful men could. Thankfully, we learned that you cannot, in fact, straight up buy the presidency if your bank account is big enough, but that doesn't mean the oxygen they took or the literal air time they ate up on TV screens couldn't have been dedicated to more representative candidates.

And that will always be the biggest shame of the 2020 Democratic primary. There are corporations, special interest groups, and individual donors, like Sheldon Adelson on the Republican side, who continue dumping money into the American political election process, backing and funding the candidates of their choice. And they aren't donating money from an altruistic impulse. They are doing it for a reason:

to ensure that their initiatives and policies are taken care of once the candidate they're backing wins office—donating hundreds of millions at a time to further their own causes in a way that typical Americans or nonwealthy candidates cannot. Why would Exxon Mobil want to invest in green technology that would reduce their profits? Obviously, they'd only want to invest in a candidate who would further their own interests. That's how the system works, and it is the antithesis of what it means to have a free and fair election.

This class divide between donors and the voters they're paying to influence has poisoned the entire American political system. The current structure of our politics allows the powerful to continue to profit from the status quo. It's of the utmost importance for voters to see and understand which candidate is in which billionaire's or corporation's pocket. That will tell you where their real agenda lies, no matter the pretty words that come out of their mouths.

By the time Senator Kamala Harris dropped out of the race at the end of 2019, before any ballots had been cast, the field of Democratic presidential hopefuls included more billionaires, like Tom Steyer, than black people.

Before even a single vote had been cast, each billionaire in the race had dropped hundreds of millions of dollars into television advertisements and staff. That money did help bump their names to the top tier and forced the media and voters to consider their candidacies—even though, in Bloomberg's case, he wasn't even trying to compete in the four early contests in Iowa, New Hampshire, Nevada, or South Carolina, which have historically set up the person who will ultimately go on to win the Democratic nomination. Their leapfrogging into the field months after the race began is one of the most obvious signs of the advantage given to the wealthy in our country.

The financial obstacles that Kamala Harris, Julián Castro, or Cory Booker faced weren't present for white men running for the same office, and that is a big problem for the future of the progressive movement. If the liberal party and voters want to see themselves represented at all levels of American government, financing it into existence is going to continue to be a huge hurdle with the current process. In the 2020 primary, candidates of color continued to drop out or struggle to qualify for the Democratic primary debates for financial reasons. It became clear that the end of white politics needs to begin with the Democratic Party's relationship to class and money in politics.

This is a matter that needs to be addressed with the utmost urgency and the sharpest focus of intent. The reality is that we live in an America where, for many qualified candidates, not receiving super PAC funding means certain campaign death. Super political action committees are a post Citizen's United phenomena; these PACs fund political advertising and lobbyists, who go to Capitol Hill to influence legislators to push or stop a piece of legislation and its contents. In today's world, super PAC donations can provide unlimited sources of funds for campaigns.

The news that Harris was suspending her presidential campaign came as a shock at the time because she was always viewed by experts as one of the democratic hopefuls with a potential to rebuild the winning and diverse Obama coalition. One wonders how a system devised to raise the voice of the people rewards billionaires over candidates of color who represent groups that are often unrepresented in

American presidential contests. In American history, Harris was only the third black woman to run for a place behind the Resolute desk in the Oval Office. Here is a moment where our country's capitalist nature has come back to haunt us, robbing us of phenomenally qualified candidates with the voice and vision to actually change our nation's politics. But then again, why would those being benefited by the system—the establishment politicians and billionaires—even want that to change, right?

Although she had strong fundraising numbers and memorable moments in the 2020 Democratic primary, Harris was unable to sustain the boosts that her debate performances gave her and turn them into campaign capital. Her exit threw the primary into chaos, turning what was once the most diverse Democratic primary field in American history into the least diverse group several months later. Even though candidates like Mayor Pete and Tom Steyer didn't make it to Super Tuesday, Harris's early exit, followed by the male candidates of color weeks later, demonstrated the hierarchy of structural challenges facing candidates who aren't straight white men. These dynamics put women and candidates of color at a disadvantage from the start; trend lines show that women and women of color have a much harder time raising money for political campaigns. It's also difficult for white women and men of color, but women of color who run have the highest bar to clear to create financially viable campaigns.

Former New York City mayor Michael Bloomberg is a prime example of the billionare advantage. A latecomer to the 2020 presidential race, Bloomberg is a moderate Democratic billionaire who ran New York City for over a decade. As a candidate, he operated from the stance that the path to victory led through reaching moderate voters who voted for President Obama in 2012 but flipped to Donald Trump in 2016. He displayed no intention whatsoever of speaking to women or voters of color in his political policy. Bloomberg's fellow billionaire Tom Steyer left the race on the night he finished third in South Carolina, and Bloomberg dropped out after Super Tuesday. But the hundreds of millions Steyer and Bloomberg spent on the race had already had the effect of pushing out candidates of color who weren't rich enough to keep up with their aggressive campaign spending.

Elizabeth Warren isn't rich either. And her campaign's refusal of corporate PAC money was an important symbolic move to set up her campaign in the way she wanted to run the country if elected. Warren's proposed wealth tax would tax the wealthy who have capital exceeding $50 million at a rate of 2 percent on the 50 millionth and first dollar, and every dollar thereafter, upsetting rich folks who are desperate to maintain their 1 percent status and tax exemptions. Billionaire candidates like Bloomberg would obviously oppose such agendas, but most importantly, it's clear what his true agenda was: getting himself into the White House using the muscle of his own bank account. This is an important distinction between him and someone like Warren (who also comes from a working-class family) because it makes him less susceptible to the public opinion checks and balances that the other, less-wealthy candidates need to survive in the race. Whereas those others have to appeal to their constituencies for votes and donor support, billionaires can carry on their own agenda without such hitches or considerations.

Corporate influence over our politics is an area where younger people can have a bigger influence on how we do

politics; they are, generally, more progressive than older generations. All the members of The Squad, including AOC, ran
campaigns without any corporate PAC donations, refusing to
be put in the pockets of corporate money that would dictate
the way they make policy. They are not pandering to lobbyists and PACs for campaign money, choosing instead to run
for higher office with a focus on grassroots campaigns.

And the flow of money into politics isn't the only morally
problematic issue we're facing in today's American system;
there's also the flow of money *out* of the people's hands and
into the hands of the already wealthy that poses a troubling
issue as well. At the same time that corporations, wealthy
private donors, and super PACs are making progressivism
an uphill battle on the political stage by choosing to only invest in candidates who will do their bidding—thus putting
the campaigns of the candidates who *won't* climb into their
pockets at a severe financial disadvantage—the same factions of people are also systematically dismantling American
labor unions. The GOP has weakened the political power
of working-class and blue-collar Americans in the United
States by electing conservative state legislators who will pro-
pose the union-gutting laws on the behalf of their corporate
masters. Concurrently, corporate influence over politics and
globalization has driven many companies out of business or
their production operations overseas.

That strain on the labor that produces everything we consume has become untenable as entire communities suffer
from economic collapse. The system feels rigged because
it *is* rigged against people who work for a living to make
money and to pay their bills. The power of labor unions to
represent their members has diminished as their jobs are

moved abroad. Labor unions, which historically allowed working-class people to reach up into the middle class with a foundation of security and health care benefits, are now weaker than ever. They can't fight for fair treatment or protect themselves when factories and plants find themselves closing, and that isn't going to change by ignoring the bad actors who are corrupting this process, intentionally weakening the economic security of everyday working people. If you're spending most of your time thinking about the money you're making off your investments or your retirement account, then you aren't who I'm talking about. Imagine a lived reality where most of your time is spent thinking about how to put food on the table for the next meal and the one after that. Imagine that such a lived reality has come to pass because your labor union, which was supposed to provide employee protection, has been dismantled at the hands of the rich and your job has now been lost. This is the reality for so many Americans across the country.

Republicans have weakened worker protections and labor unions on the state level and have passed right-to-work laws in Republican-controlled legislatures across the country. Pushed by conservatives, like the Koch brothers, through super PACs and other special interest organizations that limit the power of workers, these laws effectively ended collective bargaining rights, which is the right of groups of employees at a single company to organize and fight for their rights as workers as a group. The Supreme Court eliminated these rights when it eradicated mandatory union fees for workers along partisan lines. These new laws leave many American workers without a seat at the table and no job security or benefits. These legislative changes fundamentally changed the power that labor unions have to advocate for their members and as a mobilization force for the Democratic Party.

Conservative funders like the Koch brothers have a vested interest in maintaining the power they have by building more power and crushing the rest of us under their thumbs. They fund conservative politicians who strip away the bargaining rights that created our American middle class. They also do not have an interest in advocating for women of color who work in low-wage service jobs and who, until now, didn't have the numbers to be a transformational political force at the ballot box. This is a blatant example of how class struggles maintain the wealth gap in our country, the rich stripping the poor until they're left wholly defenseless and at the mercy of the rich.

While money in politics may not seem like an issue that everyday people need to care about, big corporate money and rich white Americans who want to keep their taxes at zero and want to maintain the status quo are funding campaigns that will do just that. The first step is to hold politicians accountable when they do let the influence of big money impact their legislation. That's an easy one. The harder step is when you need to vote out someone you may like in favor of someone else who *isn't* adhering to such corrupt practices. Multiple-term incumbent politicians are often well-liked in the communities they represent; that's one of the reasons they've been reelected so many times. But, that doesn't mean that they're working every day with their constituency's interests in mind rather than being more concerned with how to keep the donor funds flowing in to keep them in office cycle after cycle. That imbalance is reflected in the types of legislation that actually get passed and, most importantly, what is even allowed to be discussed at all. What topics are even deemed worthy of discussion is often limited by these powerful monied forces. So when we see a politician being blamed for being in the pockets of various corporations and wealthy donors, we should not turn a blind eye and excuse their behavior when it's within our voter power to simply remove them from office.

Yes, it's about class, but it's also about identity. And how much money you have, how much money you can give to campaigns, and how that money shapes the power you wield over others is a system we have to reform to make it work right. As AOC says, the new model of leadership is those who "serve the people and not the powerful"; the billionaire boys' club, or the folks who happened to have cut the biggest checks.

CONCLUSION

The Path
Forward

I THINK IT'S FATE that I found myself putting the finishing touches on the concluding chapter of *The End of White Politics* on Super Tuesday 2020. That day, March 3, 2020, will go down in American history as the day that black people sent a clear message to the white political and media establishment: the black vote is the bedrock of the Democratic party.

As I've mentioned, for the better part of over three years since the election of Donald J. Trump, political media pundits and commentators have been obsessed with the working-class white voters in Michigan, Pennsylvania, and Wisconsin, which, they assumed, hand-delivered the electoral college to our forty-fifth president. But, as you've read in these chapters, there is a lot more to the story. Those voters don't represent the bulk of the Democratic coalition of the future, which is a mix of voters of color of all generations, particularly the African American and Latino communities, as well as college-educated white women and the LGBTQ+ community, whose social and political stances have both made huge strides toward equality in the past decade while simultaneously being threatened by the Trump administration.

A large part of the premise of this book has been to force the white establishment of the American government to wake up. The old way of doing things is over. The old boys' club is over. The end of white politics is upon us, but that has never meant that white politicians *couldn't* lead a diverse coalition of the future; it's that they now have no choice but to focus on our concerns and speak to us directly as the central base of the Democratic coalition.

When I started writing this book in the summer of 2019, I didn't know that the largest and most diverse field of presidential candidates in the history of American politics would whittle down into an all-white septuagenarian field. But here we are. We have Joe Biden, seventy-seven, set to take on Donald Trump who is seventy-three years old, with Mayor Pete Buttigieg, Amy Klobuchar, Michael Bloomberg, Tom Steyer, and Elizabeth Warren dropping out of the race in the days after South Carolina's decisive primary win for Biden and Super Tuesday. And then, in the midst of the COVID-19 pandemic, Bernie Sanders dropped out, leaving Uncle Joe as the presumptive Democratic nominee for the president of the United States.

American voters must reflect on why diversity was whittled down in favor of stale pale male politics. As feminist writer Lauren Duca wrote after the last viable woman candidate, Senator Elizabeth Warren, exited the race: "I'm afraid it's too late to ask to un-see *The Matrix* now. America is an oligarchy ruled by the hierarchy of the white supremacist patriarchy, and we must each commit to a habit of political action, out of duty to ourselves and each other. At any given moment, you're either actively fighting for equality, or you're complicit in the system of oppression that prevents it."

It's not a coincidence that the female candidates and candidates of color had the most difficult time gaining traction and money to fund their campaigns. And you can't look back at what happened and not see that in the 2020 Democratic primary there were only white candidates who were left standing in the end.

This whittling down demonstrates part of the thesis of this book. The system is rigged. The majority of representation in American politics has been white, and it has been male. That's because we've centered the needs and wants of white people for too long in the United States. America is changing, and the future has to look different. The future will look different and be different to the benefit of everyone if everybody puts their collective power behind a more representative democracy. If conservative white Americans can open their eyes to see through the blinders of privilege that the policies that progressives and voters of color align on—such as health care and childcare reform, the end of police brutality, and female reproductive rights, making them safer too, and more in control of their own lives, then we will all, collectively, be a lot better off. The end of white politics post-Trump has to be an intentional act by the Democratic Party. It has to be an intentional movement to see people of color as powerful and essential components of a winning progressive coalition. Our divides on the left have led us down to an old white male for president when the electorate has never been more diverse in American history. Let's make this a wake-up call to Democratic voters everywhere.

By looking at the work of previous generations and learning from their missteps, the next generation can be even more successful in shaping the future of this country. And we'll find the light at the end of the tunnel.

Let this be the last time we do this in America. It's not a good look for a party so diverse. The 2020 Democratic primary demonstrated that we can't move forward to the future until we're willing to support and get behind the leaders we haven't seen represented in the past. Bernie is right when he says that we won't win when we do the "same old, same old politics." I'd like to add the specific caveat: the same old *white* politics.

Let *The End of White Politics* influence the Democratic Party—a party in need of a way to bridge the gap between the younger generations and those of our parents and grand-parents. The end of white politics is an unapologetic embrace of the expansion of the political conversation to include the diverse set of lived experiences that make up America and not just the limited concerns of white voters at the expense of everyone else. The time is now, and it's women and people of color who have the numbers. The power is in *our* hands.

Acknowledgments

This book wouldn't be possible without my parents Eugene and Yvette Maxwell, who taught me to question everything and stand up for anyone who had just a little less power.

I'm grateful for my sister Rebekah Maxwell and my manager Josanne Lopez for always holding me down in every single way. I want to thank my editor Krishan Trotman, who urged me to write this book at this exact time, and to my editorial partner Felice Laverne, who helped me navigate the book editing process for my first book with laughs and positivity. I'm forever inspired by my sources for the book: Stacey Abrams of Georgia, Congresswoman Ayanna Pressley of Massachusetts, and activist Bree Newsome of North Carolina.

I also want to thank my SiriusXM Progress family and Megan Lieberman and Dave Gorab. I will always love my Hillary for America Family!

I wouldn't be able to stay sane without my partners in feminism, Jess McIntosh and Samhita Mukhopadhyay. And I wouldn't be able to stay grounded without my friends for life, Jasmine Silva, Doning Barber, Silva Medina, Dr. Christina Greer, Dr. Kendra Field, and Camonghne Felix.

Notes

25   **even White House adviser Bill Moyers:** See billmoyers
.com/2014/07/02/when-the-republicans-really-were-the
-party-of-lincoln.

37   **One celebrity Bernie Sanders surrogate:** See www
.cnn.com/2016/03/29/politics /susan-sarandon-donald
-trump-hillary-clinton-bernie-sanders/index.html.

57   **During a lecture to white college:** See www.newsreel.org
/transcripts/essenblue.htm.

65   **The exchange went as follows:** As reported by Catherine
Kim for Vox, July 12, 2019.

91   **they should keep their word:** See time.com/5442702
/lauren-underwood-health-care-illinois-14.

95   **as *Fortune* magazine noted:** Melanie Eversley, "Black
Women Voters Will Be Central to the 2020 Presidential
Election, Experts Predict," *Fortune*, June 20, 2019,
https://fortune.com/2019/06/20/black-women-voters
-2020-election/.

107   **Five years after Maya Harris's paper:** Maya Harris,
"Women of Color: A Growing Force in the American
Electorate," Center for American Progress, October 30,
2014, https://www.americanprogress.org/issues/race/
reports/2014/10/30/99962/women-of-color/; **2019 report
that confirmed Harris's analysis:** Danyelle Solomon
and Conner Maxwell, "Women of Color: A Collective
Powerhouse in the U.S. Electorate," Center for American
Progress, November 19, 2019, https://www.american

progress.org/issues/race/reports/2019/11/19/477309
/women-color-collective-powerhouse-u-s-electorate/.

116 **women have a harder time:** See www.nytimes.com/2018
/10/3.

128 **This phenomenon was even covered by Bret Stephens:**
"We Need More Sister Souljah Moments," *New York Times*,
March 22, 2019.

131 **Older millennials are still recovering:** See www.business
insider.com/how-the-great-recession-affected-millennials
-2019-8.

142 **A Just Society legislation:** See ocasio-cortez.house.gov
/ajs; **ensure that we are on a path:** See ocasio-cortez
.house.gov/ajs.

153 **He warns Democrats:** The full speech is available at www.
cityclub.org/inc/audio-player.php?event_id=1302;
according to a *Washington Post* article: Matt Viser,
"Biden's Tough Talk on 1970s School Desegregation Plan
Could Get New Scrutiny in Today's Democratic Party,"
Washington Post, March 7, 2019, https://www.washington
post.com/politics/bidens-tough-talk-on-1970s-school
-desegregation-plan-could-get-new-scrutiny-in-todays
-democratic-party/2019/03/07/9115583e-3eb2-11e9-a0d3
-1210e58a94cf_story.html.

161 **characterized his response:** Katie Glueck, "Biden Has
Deep Connection to Black Voters. Will It Translate into
Votes? Opinion Today, September 15, 2019, https://
opiniontoday.com/2019/09/15/biden-has-deep-connection
-to-black-voters-will-it-translate-into-votes/.